God's People at Prayer

God's People at Prayer

A YEAR OF PRAYERS AND RESPONSES FOR WORSHIP

JOHN KILLINGER

ABINGDON PRESS / *Nashville*

GOD'S PEOPLE AT PRAYER
A YEAR OF PRAYERS AND RESPONSES FOR WORSHIP

This book is printed on acid-free paper.

Library of Congress Cataloging-in-Publication Data

Killinger, John.
  God's people at prayer : a year of prayers and responses for worship / John Killinger.
    p. cm.
  Includes index.
  ISBN 0-687-33463-2 (binding: pbk. w/ lay-flat binding : alk. paper)
  1. Church year—Prayer-books and devotions—English. I. Title.

BV30.K52 2006
264'.13—dc22

                                                          2006005001

06 07 08 09 10 11 12 13 14 15—10 9 8 7 6 5 4 3 2 1
MANUFACTURED IN THE UNITED STATES OF AMERICA

For
BOB and PIGEON HUNDLEY
with love and gratitude
for their friendship

Contents

PART TWO: Civic Holidays

PART THREE: Special Days in the Congregation

CONTENTS

Introduction

NOTHING SHAPES the devotional and theological life of a church more than the prayers offered by the minister and congregation in their hours of worship. Subtly, inevitably, our religious psyches are shaped by these conversations with God, the way stalactites and stalagmites are formed in caves by the constant dripping of water that seeps through the limestone.

Therefore it is extremely important for ministers and leaders of the congregation to pay special attention to the composition of such prayers. By so doing, they will mold the lives and attitudes of their members more in these few minutes than in all the other times combined.

From a practical standpoint, most ministers are extremely busy and often don't have adequate time to write prayers for each Sunday and special occasion themselves. I offer this volume of prayers with the hope that some of them will enrich your congregation's worship.

Or perhaps my prayers will serve as inspiration for your own prayers. During my years in ministry, I often took down from the shelves my volumes of John Baillie and William Barclay and Samuel H. Miller and read them until my spiritual imagination caught fire and I was ready to write a prayer of my own, expressing what was in my own heart and what I thought the members of my congregation wanted and needed to pray about.

There are three sections in this book, as the reader will discover: first, prayers for the usual holy days and seasons; then, prayers for the many civic holidays that are noticed or celebrated in the church; and, finally, prayers for special days in the congregation, such as Christian Education Sunday, Homecoming, and World Communion Sunday. For each special day or event, I have offered a pastoral prayer and a responsive prayer. In addition, I have suggested related passages of scripture that might be read.

However they are used in your church, these prayers and responses are offered in the hope that they will assist you and the members of your congregation toward a richer companionship with God, all "in the name of Jesus."

Part One

Holy Days
and Seasons

THE FIRST SUNDAY OF ADVENT

Pastoral Prayer

COME AGAIN, O GOD, and visit us in this world of sin and darkness with the spirit of your Son Jesus. Our hearts cry out in anguish from the suffering of masses of people—from injustice to the poor, from the inequities of medical care, from the oppression of the helpless, from the neglect and abuse of children, from the unequal distribution of wealth, from the unwillingness of governments to correct the problems, from materialism and unemployment and self-destruction and gross immorality. Only in you, O God, is there hope for this poorly governed planet. This is why our hearts leap up again at Christmas, for Christmas means candles and carols and stars and love. Christmas reminds us of the light that dawned in peasants' hearts at Bethlehem all those centuries ago, a light that will never be extinguished but will grow and grow through the centuries until your kingdom has finally and fully come on earth. Christmas reminds us of the Child who was born in a cattle stall, the Son of God arriving in very unfavorable circumstances to bless a world that was largely unaware of his coming. It is better now, O God; there are many of us who are aware of his coming again. But we have been poor stewards of the story. The world is still enthralled to darkness. People are still selfish and blind to love. Evil still thrives in our hearts and in the way people deal with one another. Show us the light again this year. Help us to see it with the eyes of those who saw the coming of Christ all those years ago. Remind us of hope and love and peace. Convert us from our dark and selfish ways into people of the kingdom, and give us a mission in the world, to make straight the ways of our Lord and to exalt the poor and unfortunate before his coming again. Teach us to sing the old songs with new zest, and to embrace the gospel with new power. For your Son is entering the world afresh and our hearts are glowing with the promise of his return. Amen.

Responsive Prayer

Leader: That first Christmas was filled with extraordinary signs, O God—the visits of angels, the promise of a Savior, the song of the expectant mother, the star that guided eastern wise men.

People: **Our lives are also filled with miracles, although we are often too busy to notice them—these marvelous bodies, so intricately made; the strange forces in the world, such as magnetism and electricity and light and power; the gifts of love and sympathy and compassion, that make life so much richer than mere physical existence.**

Leader: Teach us, O God, to see the deeper meanings of things all around us.

People: **Help us to see the angels in our lives, and to care about the things that are holy and sacred.**

Leader: Enable us to regard the coming of Christ in a new light, so that we are transformed into people of joy and passion.

People: **Grant us the most special gift of all this Christmas—a sense of your divine presence in our midst, converting everything around us into beauty and meaning. Then we shall live with new purpose, and our lives will become blessings to others. Nothing will be the same; everything will be changed. And we shall sing your praises with new voices and lift up our hearts with great joy—the true joy of Christmas! Through Jesus our Savior. Amen.**

Suggested readings: Isaiah 40:1-5; Psalm 119:89-96; John 1:19-28

THE SECOND SUNDAY OF ADVENT

Pastoral Prayer

THERE IS SOMETHING very humbling about Christmas, O God. When we remember that Christ, the Lord of all glory, was born in a simple cattle stall and laid in a manger, it affects the way we think about ourselves and our pretensions of goodness and greatness. In the scheme of eternity, O Lord, we are only grains of sand on the seashore, molecules in an ocean of churning humanity. Yet you have loved us with an infinite love, and cared for each of us as if we were the only person in the entire world. We cannot understand such a miracle, we can only accept it and live with hearts full of gratitude. Teach us in this special season, O God, to begin to love as you love, and to begin with the poorest, neediest persons we know. Help us to make a difference in the world by caring for those who are most desperate for love and companionship, those who have no power, those who are most neglected and abused by the systems we live in. Fill us with compassion. Motivate us with the example of Christ. Enable us to represent him to the best of our humble abilities. Let this be a Christmas in which we look beyond ourselves and the happiness of our families to the people around us who are in want, and to the vast world of need in the ghettos of large cities and the remote areas of desolation and the unknown regions of Third World nations. Show us how to share what we have with all of these people. Make us joyous conduits of your grace. Heal our sick, we pray, and minister to those who are lonely and depressed. Anoint our visitors with the spirit of the Christ whose birthday we shall soon celebrate. Turn this community of the faithful into a way-station for the poor, the broken, and the desperate of our own area. And let the spiritual power that resided in Christ reside in us as well, that we may honor him with our love and compassion and commitment, now and forevermore. Amen.

Responsive Prayer

Leader: Let us remain in silence for a few moments, waiting for the Spirit of the Lord to open the eyes of our hearts and reveal the things we need to know and remember. (*Silence*) Now let us speak of the things that have been revealed.

People: **Some of us have seen the foolishness of our lives, O God, and what a high price we are paying for fleeting pleasures.**

Leader: Others have recalled the way we have neglected spiritual treasures we might have had, and the gifts we have failed to provide for our friends and families.

People: **Some have realized that this is a perfect time to ask for your forgiveness and for the power to transcend the failures of our lives, so that we can begin to live each day in a state of grace and joy, making our lives count for good in the world.**

Leader: I am personally aware of the failure of our church to rise above earthly concerns and care about the things that really matter—the welfare of the poor, the joy of little children, compassion for lost and wayward people, providing a haven of comfort and strength for the broken and battered people of our society.

People: **Everything in our lives changes when we experience your presence, O God. It is all up-ended, and the things we thought were so important are no longer important at all, while the things we neglected become central to our awareness. Help us to live in this up-ended state, so that we do not lose the vision of the way life ought to be. Let this time of Christmas be the season of our renewal, so that it makes a tremendous difference in our lives. Show us the way to Bethlehem, and teach us to fall down and worship the most important Child who was ever born. For his name's sake. Amen.**

Suggested readings: Isaiah 40:6-11; Psalm 119:41-48; John 1:29-34

THE THIRD SUNDAY OF ADVENT

Pastoral Prayer

IN THE MIDST of all the preparations for Christmas, O God, the baking and decorating and shopping and partying, grant that we shall not miss the real meaning of the occasion, or a sense of the presence of Christ that we all need in such a busy, materialistic world. Teach us to find moments of spiritual depth in all the hubbub—times when we retreat from activities and pressures to contemplate the momentous birth itself and the possibility, even now, of communing with your Spirit in the swift currents of our lives. In short, help us to be still and know that you are God. Let the deeper significance of Advent and Christmas overtake us in our rush to the end of the season, and let it refashion our lives in the image of the One whose birthday we celebrate. Help us to be just and kind and thoughtful of the poor. Give us a faith that will sustain us even in the face of our own brokenness and death. Show us a vision of what life ought to be like for all the people on earth, and enlist us in the achievement of that life. Then the lights on the Christmas trees will shine even brighter for us, and our joy in the season will be more unremitting. Be especially close now to all our friends and loved ones who are experiencing difficult times for any reason—health or jobs or school or family relationships or mortality. Bless our visitors with an extra sense of your presence after being with us today. Attend to our children in this excited time of their young lives, and help them to grow in love and relationships through the special joys of Christmas. And grant that we adults may likewise come through the ordeal of busyness with a new and higher sense of what our lives ought to be—and *can* be. Through Christ our Lord. Amen.

Responsive Prayer

Leader: Sometimes, O God, we envy the people whose Christmas will be simple but intensely real, like that of the shepherds who came to visit the baby Jesus.

People: **We get too caught up in the traditions and trappings of the season, and often forget the deeper meaning of the birth of Jesus, that it was your way of saying you love us and are preparing a place for us in your eternal kingdom.**

Leader: Teach us to find rest in Christmas instead of busyness, and serenity instead of anxiety.

People: **Help us to relax, breathe deeply, and experience a sense of your holy presence in our lives.**

Leader: Let the gift of your Son, and his life and ministry, his death and resurrection, become uppermost in our lives this Christmas.

People: **And let the spirit of his life—especially his love and faithfulness to you, and his care for the poor and marginal people around him—take over our lives and transform us into true followers of his way.**

All: **Then it will truly be Christmas, and not just for a day but for the rest of our lives. In the name of the Child whose birthday we celebrate. Amen.**

Suggested readings: Isaiah 40:18-26; Psalm 119:49-56; Philippians 2:1-11

THE FOURTH SUNDAY OF ADVENT

Pastoral Prayer

IT IS ALMOST CHRISTMAS, O God, and many of us are worse for wear because of it. We have shopped and baked and gone to parties and eaten things we shouldn't and generally abandoned ourselves once again to the frenzy of the season. And those of us who haven't mailed our Christmas cards or finished our shopping or wrapped our presents are filled with anxiety about getting everything done, while those who have done these things are probably tired and still a little anxious lest they have forgotten something in all their flurry of activity. How did things get this way, dear God? How did the simple, unpretentious birth of Jesus in a cattle stall near a tenth-rate little town in the Middle East grow into such a frantic, exhausting, and budget-busting occasion as the one we celebrate today? We're not complaining. Christmas is one of the biggest joys of our existence. We love the colored lights, the evergreens, the hustle-and-bustle of the shopping malls, the frenzied baking and gift-wrapping and partying, the stories of Santa and his elves and reindeer, the excitement of little children, the air of expectation. But we do pray, O God, that we shall not lose the real meaning of Christmas under all this blanket of cultural traditions and fevered preparations. Give us some quiet moments when we commune with you and say thanks for the true spirit of the season. Help us to pause at our desks or over the cooktop or in the traffic at the mall and have a sense of your rich and abiding presence that we might not have ever known if Jesus had not been born all those years ago. And let that presence restore us to our saner minds and remind us of important interpersonal things we have to do, such as visiting a shut-in or taking a casserole to an elderly friend or being there for a person who is missing a loved one or bringing a special gift to someone who is poor and in want at this busy time of the year. Grant that the Jesus whose birth we remember at Christmas will be more than a little child for us—that he will be a living presence whose spirit is here right now to challenge our lethargy and encourage us with hope and remind us of a love that knows no boundaries of any kind. And we shall all praise you, and sing carols about your Son, with a joy that will transform even a major cultural event like this one into a time of deep spiritual sensitivity and loving celebration. Through Christ our Lord. Amen.

Responsive Prayer

Leader: It is nearly time, Lord. Christmas is almost here.

People: **It can't come too soon, O God, for our troubled and weary world. We need to hear the song of the angels again, and know that your spirit is still here in spite of war and crime and human failure.**

Leader: We pray that we won't be too tired and busy to recognize your spirit when we see it, or to hear the song of the angels when it is being sung.

People: **Give us hearts that are sensitive to everything—to the cries of hungry children, the despair of jobless people, the rebellion of teenagers, the anger of terrorists, the indifference of politicians, the hopeless plodding of millions. Let us weep over the suffering of the masses and identify with the disappointments of children. And help us to resolve to become a part of your solution to the world's problems by joining in the movement of love that began with the birth of the Child of Bethlehem.**

All: **Let love be the greatest ingredient in our Christmas this year, and let it fill our hearts to overflowing from this hour forward. We shall pay our homage to Christ by loving others as you have loved us. In his holy name. Amen.**

Suggested readings: Isaiah 40:27-31; Psalm 119:57-72; Matthew 1:18-25

CHRISTMAS EVE

Pastoral Prayer

IT IS HERE, O God; the holy time has come. We begin the cycle of Christ's birth and life and death and resurrection. Forgive the sins and self-preoccupation that have marred our coming to this hour, and take away all thoughts, cares, and ambitions that would now prevent our worshiping you. Help us to enter this moment freshly, and with full hearts, remembering how important it is to the whole world. Let the spirit that came into the world that night so long ago now enter our own spirits, converting them to its way and its will. Take away all fear and hesitance and distraction. Enable us to enter into the holy of holies with you, and to sense your presence so vividly that it will leave our lives changed and renewed. When we read about angelic choirs, let us really hear them. When we read about lowly shepherds coming to view the holy

Child, let us see the scene, let us actually feel the rarefied air of that stable, rank with the smells and sounds of cattle, warm with the fact of a human birth. Help us to bring our real selves to the experience in order that the experience may be convincingly real to us. Let the holy birth quash all thoughts of buying and wrapping presents, sending and receiving cards, and taking part in an endless round of festivities. Make the experience itself the thing, and let our participation in it transform who we are, so that we may enter your kingdom. And then let us follow the star we have seen until we arrive at all those decisions and modifications of our existence that you desire. For yours are the kingdom and the power and the glory forever. Amen.

Responsive Prayer

Leader: Let us be very still, and listen for the sound of heavenly choirs.

People: **We want to hear them, O God, and know that we are surrounded by angels.**

Leader: Let us imagine the scene in the stable, when the royal Son of God was born and laid in a manger.

People: **We want to see it, O God, even in our minds' eyes, and remember what it means that you loved the world so much that you gave your only Son to be born and to suffer and die for our sins.**

Leader: If we try very hard, we can visualize the mother of our Savior, her brow still wet with the labor of giving birth, and Joseph, his earthly father, attendant upon the holy Child.

People: **We can even see the shepherds coming in from the fields to see the little Messiah where the angels said they would find him, and imagine their whispers of wonder and awe as they beheld the little King of Kings.**

All: **It is a holy night, even all these centuries after it occurred, and our hearts are lifted up by contemplating it again, the way people's hearts have been lifted up through the centuries. Grant a blessing to the entire world, O God, for the sake of this wondrous night. Amen.**

Suggested readings: Isaiah 41:17-20; Psalm 119:105-112; Luke 2:1-14

CHRISTMAS DAY

Pastoral Prayer

THERE IS NO day more special in all the year, dear God, than this very day when we remember the birth of our Savior. Our hearts are almost too small to take it in. Our own birthdays are important to us. But the birthday of Jesus is the most important birthday in the history of the world. It is more important than the birthdays of Moses and David and Peter and Paul and Charlemagne and Joan of Arc and Shakespeare and Mozart and Napoleon and Washington and Lincoln and Florence Nightingale and Martin Luther King, Jr., and Mother Teresa all rolled into one! How can we pay homage to our Lord on this special day? By being meek and humble, as he advised? By going the second mile with those who ask anything of us? By loving our enemies and praying for those who spitefully use us? Surely by all these things, dear God. But we long to do even more. We yearn to follow him with our very lives—with our dreams and hearts' desires; with our substance and all that we have; and with the hours of our days, from now until we die. Let him be uppermost in all our thoughts. Let his words and attitudes be imprinted on our hearts. When we say his name, let our eyes light up. When we encounter the poor or the disadvantaged, let us become Christ in his stead. In short, O God, let our lives be conformed to his with such eagerness and fidelity that people will see him living through us, and have their lives touched by his the way ours have been. As the bells ring out today, let them ring not only in announcement of a birth twenty centuries ago, but of a birth that has occurred today, in our hearts. For he is the Lord of life, and we shall find our happiness in following him. Amen.

Responsive Prayer

Leader: It has come at last. Let us praise God for Christmas Day!

People: **There is no day like this one, O God, for joy and celebration in all the world.**

Leader: We join our voices with those of millions who sing his name and greet his birth.

People: **The presents have been opened. The cultural trappings are behind us. Now let us praise our Lord for coming among us, and invoke his blessed presence in all our lives.**

Leader: Teach us to be quiet and recognize the holiness of this day.

People: **Take away our sin and restore us to a right relationship with you. Let the Christ who was born at Bethlehem reign in our hearts today and for all the days to come.**

All: **Let the whole world be changed because of this day. Give us peace in our time and love in all our relationships. For yours is the kingdom forever and ever. Amen.**

Suggested readings: Isaiah 42; Psalm 121; Luke 2:15-20

A Christmas Prayer for Those Who Have Lost Loved Ones During the Past Year

Christmas hasn't been the same this year, O God. It is both sadder and deeper for us because of the loss of those we held dear. We remember their presence among us—the way they looked, the things they said, the touch of their hands, the assurances of love. Because Christmas is a time of gaiety and activity, we feel their loss more keenly now than at any other time. We recall other Christmases when they were with us. But at the same time we are more deeply aware of the spiritual nature of this season, and how you use it to address the longings of our hearts. If it were not for the birth of Jesus, we would not live in the constant hope of a higher life beyond this one. We would not know the kind of love that transcends even illness and death, and whispers of an eternal existence that will amend all sorrows and overcome all absence. Help us, at this particularly hard time of our pilgrimages, to draw upon the deep reserves of faith and confidence that we have in our hearts. Enable us to rise above the sentiment of the season, the lights and trees and festive occasions, to lay hold on the most profound truth of our religion, that Christ lives, and, because he lives, we shall live too, and all our loved ones with us. In that sense, make this the finest Christmas we have ever experienced because we are in touch with what matters most in this life. Let our grief be edged in gold, and our sorrow tinged with silver. Hold our hands in the most desperate hours, and enable us to wait for the glorious morning. For this is what we are called to. This is what life and faith are all about. Blessed be the name of the Lord. And blessed be the names of our loved ones. Through Jesus Christ, whose coming and death and resurrection we celebrate again. Amen.

A Unity Christmas Prayer for Those Whose Loved Ones Have Died During the Past Year

Give us your grace, O God, to see beyond this place and time, and therefore beyond our grief. Help us to draw upon the deep resources of our faith in you, so that we are assured of our loved ones' ongoing life in your kingdom, and of their complete happiness in the constant celebration around your blessed throne. In that way, help us not to mourn their passing, but to offer their lives gratefully to you, with the prayer that we ourselves may be strengthened for the journey that lies ahead of us. Let us live in the constant awareness of your presence with us, and of the eternal joy of those we love who are now with you. Enable us so to order the remainder of our lives on this earth that we shall make them living monuments to our dear ones and their heavenly home. Make us more loving, more forgiving, more serene, because our loved ones are with you, and because we wish to conform ourselves to the image of Christ Jesus our Lord. We pray in his name. Amen.

Suggested readings: Isaiah 9:2-7; Psalm 119:145-160; Matthew 2:1-12

EPIPHANY

Pastoral Prayer

IN A WORLD WHERE nations are always at war, O God, we pray for the coming of their leaders to Christ. As the wise men of old sought the birthplace of the Savior, let those who would influence our world today be guided by your star. Bring them to the humility of a stable filled with divine love. Make them reverent toward a Child, and toward all children, who are the promise of the future. Teach them to open their treasuries and give generously of their wealth to the poor of the earth. And when they have paid their homage, send them back "by a different way"—thoughtful, grateful, and reconstituted as those who have seen and followed a great Light. Let our own nation be recommitted to the vision of the Child laid in a manger. Forgive the gross materialism that has overtaken our culture, and the vast, unthinking secularism that has grown like a blight on all our ideals. Rekindle in us the dream of a world where the ox and the bear feed from the same trough and the lion and the lamb lie side by side in gentleness and affection. Grant that the highest insights of the Christmas season may still transform the deepest evidences of our unconverted spirits, and that even yet we shall learn to love and trust and follow your way in genuine repentance and commitment. Make this church a Christmas congregation all year long, and let the warmth and hope of this season glow in each one without fail. Let the friendliness and generosity of this time become standard for us all the time, as we are caught up more and more in the beautiful spirit of the One who was born in Bethlehem. Now let that spirit bring comfort and healing into the hearts of those who grieve or ail. Let it enter the souls of all our visitors and give them a sense of great welcome here. And grant that it may so inform our liturgy and infuse our worship that we may be as caught up in your will for us and our daily lives as those journeying wise men were in ancient times. For this is your world and we are your people, together with all your other people around the globe, now and forever. In Christ our Lord. Amen.

Responsive Prayer

Leader: Today, O God, we remember the wise men who came to see the Christ Child at his birth.

People: **We remember their gifts, and wonder what we ourselves can give.**

Leader: We think of our time, our talents, and our money.

People: **But there must be something special each of us can bring.**

Leader: Perhaps a life of renewed devotion or a special act for somebody who needs us.

People: **Whisper in my heart, O God, about the unique thing that is mine to offer.**

Leader: Help me focus on that thing and present it now as a promise to you.

People: **Then help me fulfill that promise in the days ahead, and know the joy of serving you.**

All: **For you are the Lord of all life, and we worship you by sharing ourselves in the most creative ways we can imagine. Through Christ our Lord. Amen.**

Suggested readings: 1 Kings 18:20-40; Psalm 84; Matthew 2:1-12

TRANSFIGURATION SUNDAY

Pastoral Prayer

EVERYTHING YOU TOUCH, O God, is changed. The world is different when we sense your presence. An awareness of you deeply affects our daily lives. You change our relationships with others. You heal us when we are sick. You transform our grief when we have lost loved ones. There is nothing that is not changed when you come among us. We are not surprised, therefore, by what happened to Jesus on the Mount of Transfiguration—that he became transparent in love and majesty and his garments glowed with holiness. It was only one more sign of your incredible power and your transforming grace. Teach us to live in that power and grace, O God. Enable us to dwell in such constant awareness of your Spirit that our normal existence is irradiated by your love and joy and hope. Show us how to leave behind our old, worldly lives and participate each day in the greater energy and higher calling of a life of beautiful devotion. Let us truly love others more than we love ourselves, and seek the good of all your humblest servants ahead of our personal welfare. Then we shall experience the same power and invulnerability as Jesus, who, though they could kill his body, triumphed over lust and greed, betrayal and death. Make this church a fellowship of transfiguration, so that all who share our love and worship will be changed by it, glorifying your name to the uttermost parts of the earth. Grant that we may become agents of change in our community, bringing respect and justice to all who have been abused, neglected, or disenfranchised. Reach out through us to heal those who are hurt and lonely, and to free those who are imprisoned by systems or circumstances beyond their control. Let this be a day when we all go to the mountaintop with Jesus and behold a vision that will alter our way of looking at things for the rest of our lives; for you are a God who not only transcends all human limitations and imperfections, but who helps us transcend them as well. Through Christ our Lord. Amen.

Responsive Prayer

Leader: There are difficult times, O God.

People: **There are days when we don't think we can make it.**

Leader: These are the times when we need you most.

People: **These are the occasions when we'd give anything for some assurance of divine favor.**

Leader: We want to see your face or feel the touch of your hand.

People: **We long for some evidence of your presence, or even of your existence.**

Leader: Teach us how to see and feel you, O God.

People: **Show us how to react spiritually to the worst times and experiences of our lives.**

Leader: Help us to know you anywhere, and under any circumstances.

People: **Take away our blindness and lift the dullness from our hearts.**

Leader: For you are God, and you alone make our lives worthwhile.

People: **We praise you for your great glory, and seek your face as the answer to all our problems.**

Leader: Hear us and answer us, O God; help us to see you in all the affairs of our lives.

All: **For you are God, and you alone bring holiness and meaning to a world that is barren without you! Amen.**

Suggested readings: Exodus 3:1-15; Isaiah 6:1-8; Luke 9:28-36

ASH WEDNESDAY

Pastoral Prayer

DUST AND ASHES, Lord. It is hard for us to remember, when things are going well, that the grave is our destiny. That all the vigor we have known, the exuberance at games and athletics, the energy for working and creating and making love, the joy of life itself, will one day be dismissed by death. If we did remember, perhaps we would live more sensitively and think more frequently about eternal life. Forgive us for being complicit in a culture that thinks only of the moment, and steeps itself in the pleasures of the flesh. Teach us to take the long view. Help us to see things in their totality, and adjust our lives accordingly. Grant that as we begin this timely pilgrimage toward Easter we may reflect deeply on the nature of human existence and its fragility. Remind us of Jesus and his faithfulness to the things he could not see with his eyes. Let us walk with him in the valley of the shadow of death and repent of our casual attitude toward sin. Command our commitments again, O God, and let us declare ourselves to be his followers. Enable us to lay aside every weight that hinders us and walk with devotion in his footsteps. Expose our shortcomings to us, and help us to meditate on them in true repentance. Draw us into a more heavenly way, and let us rediscover the meaning of love and grace and acceptance. For we pray in the name of the One who came this way before, and, seeing what we often fail to see, bore his sufferings with courage and equanimity. Amen.

Responsive Prayer

Leader: We are standing once more at the beginning of a holy journey.

People: **It is a journey we have been waiting to make, and a journey we need to make.**

Leader: Help us, O God, to be attentive to it, marking the sins we carry with us and the temptations that line the way.

People: **Lead us, O God, into a deeper and truer commitment to you and to the values and understandings cherished by our Lord Jesus Christ.**

Leader: Enable us to reflect on the way we have lived and the way we ought to be living.

People: **Guide us once more to the life-changing decisions that await us, and give us the desire and the courage to make them. Show us how to truly love one another, and to express our love for you by caring for the most broken members of our society.**

Leader: Help us to make this a real season of prayer, and seek your heavenly assistance in overcoming the inertia that could prevent this from being a time of renewal and discovery in our lives.

People: **Send your Holy Spirit upon us, and baptize us in your divine presence, that this may be more than a span of time on the institutional calendar—that it may become a journey to new life and understanding.**

All: **Through Christ, who pioneered this way and is able to lead us as no earthly leader is able to do. Amen.**

Suggested readings: Exodus 20:1-21; Psalm 51:1-14; Matthew 25:1-13

THE FIRST SUNDAY IN LENT

Pastoral Prayer

WE HAVE BEGUN an important journey, dear God, from the valleys of human selfishness and greed to the mountaintops of spiritual presence and illumination. We know it is important because we feel the need for something new and restorative in our lives. Many of us have capitulated to the culture we live in—to the noise and pace and materialism of those whose spiritual roots do not go very deep and whose mood is often affected by the vicissitudes of the marketplace and world affairs and the latest trends. We feel shallow and fragile, and our resources for dealing with the unexpected are almost exhausted. Forgive us, O God, for being so human—for neglecting the disciplines of prayer and meditation that might have made us stronger, and for following the path of least resistance and greatest immediate pleasure. Help us this time to make this important journey as if it were our last opportunity—because for some of us that might be true. We may never live through another Lenten season. Show us how to walk with Christ as he faced his coming death in Jerusalem. Enable us to hear his words of caution and encouragement. Increase our sense of communion with him as he spent time with his disciples. Make us courageous to face our own crosses and our own important decisions. And in the end grant us an experience of resurrection from the dead—from all our old dreams and ambitions, all our tawdry allegiances, all our failed commitments and bad experiences. In short, let this be for each of us a pilgrimage of renewal and hope, so that we come at last to new resolutions and new directions for our lives. We ask this for our visitors as well as ourselves, and especially for every person who is experiencing grief, remorse, or depression today. Be God in our midst, and help us to know it. Let your glory overpower our ordinary sensibilities, and let Christ remaster our existence. Take us by the hand, and lead us on high. For yours are the kingdom and the power and the glory forever. Amen.

Responsive Prayer

Leader: This is a remarkable time, O God, and a very important one in our lives.

People: **We are greatly in need of your guidance. Our world is riddled with greed and hate and confusion. Our sensibilities are overcrowded. We seldom know the best thing to do. Our souls crave something better.**

Leader: Help us to begin a journey with you today, O God, that will carry us to new hope and understandings in Christ.

People: **Show us how to commit ourselves to you in our hearts. Help us to wait before you until we see things more clearly. Then enable us to make the right decisions and do the things we ought to do.**

Leader: Teach us how to find love again—to realize more fully how much you love us and to experience how wonderful it is to love others with a great, overwhelming love.

People: **Teach us how to take even tiny steps as we begin this journey, and then larger ones as we go along. Make the way plain to us, and help us to trust you even at the darkest times.**

All: **For you are our God, and we know that you are able to help us and keep us at all times, and to restore us to new life, through Jesus Christ our Lord. Amen.**

Suggested readings: Genesis 46:1-7; Psalm 22:1-11; Mark 7:1-16

THE SECOND SUNDAY IN LENT

Pastoral Prayer

IT IS HARD FOR us to imagine, O God, what a tidal wave of prayer and repentance is going on around the globe today because we are in the midst of the Lenten season. What a difference it could make in our dispirited, war-weary world! What a difference it could make in our lives to be a part of it! Help us to sense its importance to us, and to make this an intentional time of prayer and renewal, both for us individually and for our homes and church and community. Teach us all over again how to pray and seek your face. Enable us to put away our doubt and cynicism, our apathy and unbelief, and to immerse ourselves in your Spirit with a freshness and enthusiasm that will transform our very beings. We don't ask for any special signs of favor—only for a deep, personal sense of your presence. That in itself will change the way we regard ourselves and the world around us. That in itself will be our salvation in a time of dryness and need. Grant this same blessing to all our visitors, we pray, and to young and old alike. Let a fresh wind of spirit blow through our lives, awakening hope and energy. Show us how to love one another again, and more deeply than ever. Revive our marriages, our friendships, and all our good relationships. Restore our church to its calling in Christ. Help us to rise above prejudice and pettiness, and reclaim our mission in the world. Let us become a part of the tidal wave, and be saved in the process. We pray in the name of Christ our Redeemer. Amen.

Responsive Prayer

Leader: In your presence, O God, we become aware of how unworthy we are even to call upon your name.

People: **We have sinned, and done that which was evil in your sight.**

Leader: We have chosen the paths of least resistance, and fallen into temptation.

People: **We have failed to be the dedicated followers of Christ we intended to be. We have fallen short of our Lord's expectations for us.**

Leader: Hear our prayer of confession, O God, and restore a new spirit within us.

People: **Teach us once more to walk in the way of righteousness, and to live in a spirit of love and acceptance with all people.**

Leader: Bind up our wounds, correct our courses, and be present to us on our journeys.

People: **Let the spirit of Christ become our spirit, and let the way of the Cross become our way, in order that we may do what is pleasing in your sight,**

All: **O Lord our God, our strength and our redeemer. Amen.**

Suggested readings: Numbers 14:1-12; Psalm 63; Matthew 12:33-37

THE THIRD SUNDAY IN LENT

Pastoral Prayer

THERE IS NOTHING in the world that tests us, O God, like being alone in your presence. Then we know there is no place to hide and there is no point in pretending. You see the secrets of our hearts. You know the shortcomings of our lives. Your love and holiness discern everything about us. We *are* alone with you, O God. Each of us is alone with you right now. Help us to sense it and not to be afraid. Enable us to feel your majesty and your glory. And at the same time let us experience your love and tenderness toward us. We cannot really know you this way, O God, and not be changed. Something happens to us in your presence. We understand what we were supposed to be. We see what we have to do. The whole world looks different to us from here. Everything is trans-formed—including us. Don't let us lose this moment, O God. Enable us to grasp it and hold on to it. Let it continue to affect our lives when we leave here, when we return to our homes, when we go back to school or to work, when we encounter the people who weren't here with us. Make us witnesses to the grace we have experienced. Let it shine from our hearts and our faces. And let the whole world be different because of the time we have had with you. Through Christ, our living Savior. Amen.

Responsive Prayer

Leader: We are here, O God, because we need you.

People: **We need your strength, we need your love, we need your forgiveness.**

Leader: Help us to surrender ourselves to you so completely that our hearts can understand what you want to tell us.

People: **Speak to us about the things we need to do for you and your kingdom, about all the people we should be loving and helping, about the joy that we will feel when we are living in the center of your will.**

Leader: Let the power of your presence cleanse us and then use us.

People: **Make us real disciples of Jesus, who are willing to defy a cross for the sake of the people we need to serve, and who will experience his resurrection after the darkness.**

All: **We ask this in his name and for his sake. Amen.**

Suggested readings: Job 40:1-14; Psalm 37:1-11; Mark 12:1-12

THE FOURTH SUNDAY IN LENT

Pastoral Prayer

JESUS KNEW HE would encounter trouble when he went to Jerusalem, O God. He realized he would probably die in his clash with the elders of his faith. We would like to have his courage and strength of will in our own lives. We would like to believe so powerfully, so completely, that we could walk into the teeth of death. We would like to be so sure of our mission, so convinced of the truth, that we would do literally anything to serve you. We pray that you will help us to reach the point in our faith where we both know what you want us to do and have the determination to do it. Help us to matter—to our friends and families, to our church, to our community, to the world. Cultivate a sense of your Spirit within us. Surround us with the people and ideas and influences that will mold us into fervent followers of Jesus. Let the mind that was in him become our mind as well, so that we think the way he would think and behave the way he would behave. Teach us to care for your little ones, wherever they are, and to use everything in our means to help them. If there are people here in this room today who need our assistance in any way, lead us to them and reveal what we can do for them. Let our faith become more than an idea to us—let it be real, let it be true, let it take over our lives every day that we live. Grant that this church may be a fellowship of the truly redeemed, the people who have been transformed by the inward presence of Christ, so that we will seek not to be served but to serve, not to be loved but to love, not to be appreciated but to appreciate others. And we shall give you the honor and glory forever, through Christ our Lord. Amen.

Responsive Prayer

Leader: We often pray that you will speak to us, Lord, and then don't listen.

People: **We pray to know your will, and then won't do it.**

Leader: We ask you to come into our lives, but don't open the door.

People: **Help us to become sincere, Lord. Forgive us for trying to fool everybody, including ourselves, and help us to become honest followers of Christ. Let us care more about him and his kingdom than we do about all the things that presently interest us, such as our money, our jobs, and our pleasures.**

Leader: Teach us to walk in his way and do the things he has told us to do, in order that we may witness more effectively to our faith.

People: **Grant that every day may become the day of our salvation, and every path the path that leads us to you.**

All: **Then we shall praise you with our whole hearts, and rejoice in the unity of our souls. In the name of Christ. Amen.**

Suggested readings: Ezekiel 24:1-14; Psalm 94:1-15; Matthew 18:1-14

THE FIFTH SUNDAY IN LENT

Pastoral Prayer

FOR WEEKS NOW, O God, we have been drawing nearer to Good Friday and Easter—nearer to the crucifixion and resurrection of our Lord. It is a good journey, and a hard one. Some of us have been more serious about it than others. Help us all, we pray, to sense the importance of the journey. And even if we haven't been making it—haven't been intentionally praying and meditating about the life of Jesus and how it has shaped our history and our consciousness—we ask that we may join it now. Forgive whatever in us is unworthy of him. Draw us near to you in our spirits. Help us to forsake anything that we know is keeping us from being more filled with your life and Spirit. Pull at the tabs of our lives until we open up to you and your kingdom, until we can no longer keep to ourselves and go our own ways. Speak to us of what it would mean to us personally to become more involved with your kingdom—how we would find the peace and serenity we have always sought, how we would feel fulfilled in your love and service, how our lives would change to reflect your own great holiness and joy. The world is too shallow and fickle to satisfy us, O Lord. Only your depth of being can do that. Draw us near to you now and transform us by your presence, and we shall learn to honor you in everything we say and do, through Christ our Lord. Amen.

Responsive Prayer

Leader: You have been waiting for us, O God, all of our lives.

People: **We would never have had the patience you have had with us. We would have forsaken us long ago. In fact, some of us have already done that. We have lost all confidence in our own worth and promise.**

Leader: But you, O God, have not forsaken us. You have continued to love us and invite us into your kingdom.

People: **You have been so good to us, and blessed us in so many ways, that we have actually failed to notice.**

Leader: Forgive us, O God, and draw us into your way at last. Help us to find peace and salvation in your loving arms.

People: **Grant us a new opportunity to follow Christ and prove our faithfulness to him.**

All: **Then we shall praise you for your steadfastness, and for the love that would not let us go. For you are merciful to a fault, and forgiving beyond all imagination. Amen.**

Suggested readings: Hosea 11:1-9; Psalm 71:12-19; Luke 7:36-50

PALM SUNDAY

Pastoral Prayer

CHEERLEADERS! They were hard at work when Jesus entered Jerusalem, weren't they, O God? Everybody was happy. They had a Messiah. God was favoring them. Everything was going their way. So they called out, "Hosanna, blessed is he who comes in the name of the Lord!" It was a natural thing to do. We're the same, Lord. We too find it easy to cheer when things are going well. It's on the dark days when it's harder. The days when nothing seems to go right, when life seems dull and heavy. Days when we're sick or lose our jobs or fail a test or have a quarrel we didn't want to have. Then we don't remember to cheer very much. Then we feel more like Job's wife: "Curse God and die." It's a lot harder to be cheerful on days when we're feeling crucified, when all the fun has gone out of life and we're alone with our problems. Revive our spirits this week, O God. Remind us of your faithfulness even on the dark days—even when we feel abandoned. Help us to be steady in all kinds of days. To wait on you in the hardest of times. To know you are there, and that you care, and that joy returns with the morning. Forgive our times of doubt and our failures of nerve. Renew our faith and teach us to believe at all times, whether everybody is cheering or everybody has forsaken us. Let us move on faithfully with Christ, caring more for truth and honor and love and devotion than we do for applause or accolades. And grant that this church may always be a place of refuge and encouragement for everyone who comes here, and for all our members, whose hands and hearts are joined even when they are apart. Touch us with healing and with hope. Let peace—rich, lugubrious peace—attend us all the days of our lives. Through the Christ of triumph and of pain. Amen.

Responsive Prayer

Leader: There is a murmur of excitement in our hearts today, O God.

People: **We are entering Holy Week, and our thoughts are upon the conquering Savior.**

Leader: We like the pageantry of Palm Sunday, and the idea of welcoming Christ into the life of our community.

People: **There is always something upbeat about this day, when even the little children sing "Hosanna" and their parents echo "Blessed is he who comes in the name of the Lord!"**

Leader: But we know that darker, more somber days lie ahead of us, and the shadowy hours of Good Friday.

People: **All life is that way, dear God—bright days and hard days. Show us how to remain steady and faithful through all of them, and to praise you with a quiet, unwavering will to follow Jesus, even in the darkest of times.**

All: **Let us follow him through this week, with all its reminders of betrayed love and crucifixion, that we may worship you in gladness of heart on Easter Day. Through Christ our Lord. Amen.**

Suggested readings: Joel 2:1-14; Psalm 98; Matthew 21:1-13

HOLY THURSDAY

Pastoral Prayer

WE KNOW THERE is a shadow side to all human existence, O God, and today, especially, we are reminded of that. We like to imagine ourselves as warm and generous and loving; but there is also a part of us that is dark and resentful. We are usually upright and good; but there is an aspect of us that is sometimes devious and immoral. We are normally faithful and devoted; but we can also be unfaithful and rebellious. On the whole, we admire truth and honesty; but we are also given to lying and deceiving. We want others to see us as caring and supportive; but we can be very selfish and controlling. We have promised to follow Christ; but we often fail and follow our own desires. Teach us not to despair about this flaw in our characters, any more than Christ despaired of it in his followers. He knew their darker sides and loved them in spite of it. He reminded them that they would be unfaithful—that Judas would betray him and Peter would deny him. Yet he never disowned them or forsook them. Help us to regard the shadow side of our beings the way he did—as an inseparable part of who we are—and not to disown them. But help us also, as Christ did, to encourage the other side of ourselves, the part that responds to the light and loves the light and follows the light. And we shall praise you even with the darker sides of our natures, for you always deal with us in love and mercy. Through Christ our Lord. Amen.

Responsive Prayer

Leader: There is a part of Judas in every one of us.

People: We hate to admit it, but it is true.

Leader: Even when we try to follow Jesus, we consort with the enemy.

29

People: **Most of us are willing to sell him out if the price is high enough.**

Leader: It makes him sad, but he allows us to do what we think we have to do.

People: **He lets us seek our own destruction, even though it means crucifying him.**

Leader: Still, he forgives us and seeks our restoration.

People: **He continues to love us in spite of ourselves.**

Leader: What can we do to honor him now, despite our natures?

People: **We can apologize and ask for forgiveness; we can renew our love and rebuild our relationship with him.**

Leader: We can agree to put the kingdom of God first in our lives.

People: **We can live in daily awareness of our Judas-nature and seek to overcome it with the help of God's Spirit.**

Leader: Then surely goodness and mercy will follow us all the days of our lives.

People: **And we shall dwell in the house of the Lord forever.**

All: **Amen.**

Suggested readings: Malachi 4; Psalm 134; Luke 22:14-23

GOOD FRIDAY

Pastoral Prayer

SOMETIMES WE FORGET, dear God, that when our side of the world is bathed in sunlight, the other side is in darkness. And there is a shadow side to all of life. It would be unrealistic for us to expect light and bliss every hour of every day. Help us now to wait in darkness before the cross of Jesus. In many ways, it was the darkest hour in the history of the world. The best man who ever lived—the wisest, holiest, and most just—was put to death in the cruelest and most humiliating manner we can imagine. He never sought anything for himself. Everything he did was for others. His greatest dream was of a kingdom where the poor would dine with the rich and the lowly would enjoy the company of the finest. And he was killed for that dream by people who may have admired it but didn't share it. He constituted a threat to the security of their kind of world, where everything is skewed and compromised and unfair. Help us to mourn that today—not for his sake, but for our sakes, and for the world's sake. We too have taken up his dream of a kingdom, and it hurts us that that kingdom isn't here yet. Even those of us who profess it have our own shadow sides. We betray him and desert him just as his first disciples did. We cower when we are afraid, and don't stand up for love and justice and generosity the way he did. Forgive us, O God; this is a time for mourning—for mourning his death—for mourning the failure of his followers—for mourning the shortcomings of the church—for mourning our own lack of faithfulness and courage when the chips are down. Heal our shadow sides, O God. Bathe us in so much light from your presence that we can no longer be dark or even mournful. Let our mourning be so deep and so penetrating that it may touch the very heart and core of life itself, and change us into joyous, faithful followers. In the name of Jesus the crucified. Amen.

Responsive Prayer

Leader: This is the darkest, most somber of days.

People: **It is the day when we remember our Savior's death, and the terrible pain and suffering he endured for the sins of the world.**

Leader: We identify with him, O God, because his suffering was so real and unforgettable.

People: **The nails in his hands. The great, spiky thorns on his head. The pull of gravity on his body. The isolation and humiliation!**

Leader: We can only pray for forgiveness, O God; we feel as guilty as if we had been there.

People: **Help us to live more worthily because of him. Show us how to truly love one another, and to share what we have with the poor. Save us from being like his enemies and help us to live as his friends.**

All: **For when we contemplate him and his death, there is nothing we want more than to follow him and be like him until we all break bread and drink wine with him in your eternal kingdom. For his name's sake. Amen.**

Suggested readings: Joel 1:13–2:2; Psalm 22:14-21; Luke 22:33-38

EASTER VIGIL

Pastoral Prayer

ID JESUS' DISCIPLES have any hope on the night before they discovered that his tomb was empty, O God, or were they swathed in doubt and despair? We can't imagine what it must have been like for them. For here we are, having observed another Lenten season and paid tribute to the Cross on Good Friday, and we know that tomorrow will be Easter Day, when Christians all over the world will celebrate the resurrection of our Lord. But for a minute, dear God, help us to feel what they felt, and be stunned by the darkness and emptiness of the hours after the crucifixion. Let us experience the torpor and despair in order to transcend them in the realization of what you have done in Christ Jesus, and be ready truly to celebrate Easter. We are still afraid of death. Our culture attempts to disguise it and ignore it, but it is all around us. Our bodies are dying. Our flesh. Yet death has lost its sting in the victory of your Son over what happened to him on the Cross. You brought a new order, a new hope, into the world that day. You cancelled death's power and dominion. Now, although we are afraid, we live with hope. Hope that we shall be raised up with Christ in a realm of life and light that would be utterly blinding if we could see it now. Forgive us, O God, for the scales that grow across our eyes and hearts, so that we fail to see what you have prepared for us. And let this Easter be a time of unveiling for us, when we shall remember and see with a clarity greater than any we've ever had. For you dwell in light and your kingdom is forever. Through Christ our Savior. Amen.

Responsive Prayer

Leader: This is a special night, O God, and we can feel the excitement of it.

People: **We await the glory and power of Easter, when all Christendom celebrates the raising of Christ.**

Leader: It is important to us for how it affects our lives. Christ's resurrection means new life for us.

People: **Without it, we would be lost in sin and darkness, and there would be no hope beyond the grave.**

Leader: Grant that the beauty and thrill of the day that is about to dawn will not be lost when the day is over, but will remain with us forever as a part of our way of understanding everything.

People: **Teach us to concentrate on your presence every day that we live, and so have Easter all the time. Let your Spirit reign in our hearts forever.**

All: **For you are truly the Lord of life, and we cannot imagine our existence without you. Amen.**

Suggested readings: Job 4:12-17; Psalm 25:1-10; Luke 23:50–24:9

EASTER

Pastoral Prayer

WORDS ARE INADEQUATE for this day, O God. Images are much better: the empty tomb, the folded graveclothes, Mary Magdalene in the garden, Jesus asking her why she is weeping, her recognition of him and attempt to embrace him. It is all very surreal and dreamlike. Yet it reminds us of the greatest truth of our lives, that we were not born to live and die without hope, that there is a life above and beyond this one so beautifully idyllic that we can scarcely imagine it now. Help us to keep the images in the foreground of our consciousness, dear God; for when we forget them we succumb to the hollowness and emptiness of the culture around us. We begin to doubt and to fear and to become as hopelessly materialistic as the rest of the world. Renew our faith today, O God. Draw us back into the way of Jesus—the way of love and service and self-discipline and devotion. Teach us to set our feet where his feet have walked. Lead us to the homes of the poor and friendless. Help us to take up the causes of the powerless. Let us go where he would go and do what he would do—not for honor or glory or even self- satisfaction, but because he would want it and expects us to follow him there. Shatter our complacency the way your power rolled away the stone from his grave, and let us step forth into the world with the confidence to change the human situation. Grant that we may experience healing in his name, and not healing only, but renewal and rededication, and the kind of deep peace and joy that will constantly refurbish us in the battle against evil and ignorance. Let the Christ who reigned triumphant on that first Easter Day reign triumphantly in our hearts from this day forth, and let us honor him with the very substance of our lives, now and forever. For nothing less will make us happy or satisfy the demands of your kingdom. Amen.

Responsive Prayer

Leader: This is the highest day of the year, when we celebrate the victory of Christ over death and despair.

People: **We cannot imagine a more important occasion, O God; everything else pales beside it.**

Leader: As this day changed everything about human history, dear Lord, help it to work its changes on us as well.

People: **Transform us in the image of Christ, and grant that we may see all of life from a different vantage point.**

Leader: Make us more aware of our sins and more eager to do your will in our daily existence.

People: **Convert the very desires of our hearts, so that we no longer live for ourselves but for others. Make us good and generous and loving, and help us to find joy in the simplest things.**

All: **Let the power of Christ flow through us to the world, that it may bless everyone and every place we know. For his name's sake. Amen.**

Suggested readings: Micah 2:12-13; Psalm 145:1-14; Acts 2:22-28

THE SUNDAY AFTER EASTER

Pastoral Prayer

SOMETIMES, O God, this day is called Low Sunday because it is the Sunday after Easter, when the crowds are smaller—even the choir!—and everything seems less exciting. But we realize that if we really understood what Easter was about, and how the power of Christ is still in the world today, there can never be a low or disappointing Sunday, because your Spirit has been poured into the world so lavishly and so universally that every day is actually an Easter Day to every one of us. Forgive us if we have failed to see this and have surrendered—even for a moment—to the dullness and despair to which human souls are prone. Help us to live each day on tiptoe, exulting in your presence, feeling good and expansive, and shedding blessings wherever we go, the way a shaggy old sheep sheds its wool on the bushes and pasture around it. Empower us to bring healing and encouragement to others. Teach us to share the many gifts you give us—our homes, our food, our love, our financial means, our enthusiasm for Christ and his way. Turn us into kingdom people, whose highest aim is to know and do your will with who we are and what we have. Let this church be a kingdom church, totally dedicated to you and what you want us to be. Grant that all churches everywhere may feel a sense of Easter power in their services today, and that we will no longer do business as usual, or even think of the church as a kind of business, but that we will be your eager and unfailing servants in the war against evil and poverty and ignorance and intolerance in the world. Make us fearless and imaginative. And above all make us kind and loving, in order that we may truly represent you and what you are about. Through Jesus Christ our Lord. Amen.

Responsive Prayer

Leader: Jesus was raised from the dead, the first fruits of those that slept.

People: **He is the one the church is about, and it is him we praise and adore for what the Father accomplished through him.**

Leader: You have first claim on our lives, O God, because Christ has died for our sins and you have raised him up to eternal life.

People: **We want it to mean something that we have eternal life through him. We want it to change the way we live now, so that everything we say and do is significantly different because of him. Help us to think and behave differently because we are his followers, and grant that this church may be a fellowship of those who have been transformed and are still being transformed by your divine grace. Let the power of Easter flow in us and through us to the world around us, making new disciples and inviting the world to a new and higher way of living together.**

All: **Through Christ our Savior. Amen.**

Suggested readings: Isaiah 66:1-2, 10-13; Psalm 150; Romans 8:28-39

ASCENSION SUNDAY

Pastoral Prayer

ON THIS SUNDAY, O God, we honor our Savior's return to heaven after his remarkable ministry on earth. He promised that he would sit on your right hand until the end of time. That is a great comfort to us, for it acknowledges your divine justice for those who have served you and have been persecuted for their faith. We pray for there to be more justice on earth, dear God—for your kingdom to come here as it is in heaven. We ask for your vindication of the poor, the diseased, the lonely, the outcast—and for our own involvement in their welfare. You have blessed us beyond any other people in the history of the earth—with homes and food and political stability and electrical power and modern conveniences and medical treatment and almost everything we can imagine to wish for. Grant that we may regard all these things as a mere trust, as gifts we should share with a less privileged world. Teach us to care about people in neighborhoods less safe and pleasant than our own, and those who work in jobs less rewarding and prestigious than our own. Implant in us a desire to help others by whatever means we have at our disposal. Give us a vision of your kingdom that will motivate us to make the world a better place for all its citizens, and not only those who belong to our political clubs or churches or ideologies. Let Christ, who reigns at your right hand, reign in our hearts as well, that his name may be praised wherever men and women dwell, by the power of your Holy Spirit. Amen.

Responsive Prayer

Leader: Christ is risen, O God, and returned to your side. That is the single most important fact in human history.

People: **It is more important than the discovery of fire or the wheel or the mechanical engine. It is more important than the harnessing of electricity or the splitting of the atom.**

Leader: Help us, as Christians, to remember this and to have a proper sense of respect for our own theological understanding of things.

People: **Grant that we may follow Christ in our daily lives and glorify his kingdom by the way we think and act. Let his teachings be uppermost in our minds, and his love our guide in everything.**

Leader: Make us his effective disciples in the age in which we live, in order that his life and ministry may continue in the world today.

People: **Let us crown him with our own love and devotion, and help him to become the Lord of all among the nations of the earth.**

All: **For worthy is the Lamb that was slain, and now reigns above with you in the heavens for all eternity. Amen.**

Suggested readings: 2 Kings 2:1-18; Psalm 107:1-9; Acts 1:6-11

PENTECOST SUNDAY

Pastoral Prayer

WE MARVEL AT that first Pentecostal experience, O God, when tongues of flame sat upon the foreheads of believers and they understood one another even when they didn't share a common language. What a powerful, unforgettable time it must have been for the early disciples. And yet your Spirit has never ceased to come upon followers, and your power to understand has never been withdrawn. We pray that we too may have a Pentecostal experience, dear God—a clear sense of your power in us and the joy of communing with other Christians around the world. Grant that we may never come together as a community without feeling your presence here, and that we may never differ so much in our personalities or politics or ideologies that we shall not truly love and respect one another's viewpoints. Let the peace and empowerment of Christ be upon us as a church, and transform our lives from those of isolated, unrepentant souls into those of loving, sharing, harmonious brothers and sisters. Grant that there may be concord and good will among all churches, and that together we may witness to a world that is crying out for love and togetherness. Let the gift that those early disciples released upon the world around them become our gift as well, that this time too may be an age of the Spirit and spiritual power. Bless each one of us here today—certainly including all our friends and visitors—and help us to take from this time together a share of your outpouring upon us, as though we carried living coals back to our own homes and places of business, so that the joy of this time may be spread in a wider circle. Through Christ our Savior. Amen.

Responsive Prayer

Leader: O God, who revealed your power to the early Christians as tongues of fire and common understanding,

People: **Come now and empower us as well, baptizing us in the glow of spiritual recognition and the kind of love and acceptance that will enable us to understand one another's hearts and minds.**

Leader: Rekindle our faith with such strength and enthusiasm that we shall be transformed for living and for sharing our faith with others.

People: **Let the Spirit that galvanized the early church galvanize us as well, that we may recognize the mission field around us and reach out to those who don't yet know the gospel of our Christ or how to live in peace and joy with others. Make us channels of your grace to the people of our time and culture.**

All: **And let Christ be glorified in us, today as in the days of old. For his name's sake. Amen.**

Suggested readings: Joel 2:26-29; Psalm 135:13-21; Acts 2:32-42

TRINITY SUNDAY

Pastoral Prayer

TODAY IS TRINITY Sunday on our calendar, O God, a day when we recognize the classical formulation of your nature as Father, Son, and Holy Spirit. We are humble Christians and do not always understand the depth of meaning in old theological doctrines. Yet we have experienced you in three ways in our own lives—as our heavenly Father, who watches over us and hears our prayers; as our Lord Jesus Christ, who taught us most of what we know about you and died for our sins; and as your Holy Spirit, who is still at work in the world creating what is best and most meaningful in it and encouraging us to live in the way of your kingdom. We praise you for these various ways in which we know you, and for the church, which through the ages has attempted to clarify our human experience of you and help us to make sense of such inter-relationships. Teach us to be more sensitive about these matters, and to care about their meanings. As children grow and learn more and more about the parents who have borne and kept them, help us to learn more about you and appreciate the aspects of your being and your provision for us. And as we learn more about you, help us to care more about the world you have made and your other children in the world. Make us more keenly aware of the hurt and poverty in the world, of the people who are isolated and lonely, of those who live under the curse of disease and malformation, of those whose whole existence has been marginalized by where they were born and what kind of homes they come from. Show us what to do with our resources, so that at the end of our lives we shall be happy with how we have used them and not be like the man with one talent who went out and buried it because he feared his master. Let our souls reflect the amplitude of the Trinity itself, and let our hearts be inclined to you at all times. For you are our God, Father, Son, and Holy Spirit, and we adore you as the giver and sustainer of all life. Amen.

Responsive Prayer

Leader: On this day we honor the Trinity—God the Father, Jesus the Son, and the Holy Spirit.

People: **Grant, O God, that this may be more than a formula in our church—that it may truly reflect our broad experience of you and the way in which you have revealed yourself to us across the years.**

Leader: We have a single set of parents; and yet they love us and minister to us in different ways.

People: **So it is with you, O God; you care for us as our Father, you shared yourself with us as our Savior, and you lead us every day as the Holy Spirit. We are grateful for the fullness of your care for us, that meets our needs in these different ways. Teach us to respond to your care with adoration and faithfulness, and grant that we may be your loving servants all the days of our lives.**

All: **In the name of the blessed Trinity, Father, Son, and Holy Spirit. Amen.**

Suggested readings: Genesis 1:1-8; Proverbs 8:22-36; John 1:1-14

REFORMATION SUNDAY

Pastoral Prayer

THERE IS ALMOST nothing we ever do, O God, that is harder than reordering or remaking ourselves. Yet there are times, both in our own lives and in the life of the church, when that is the only way we can be faithful to you. Today we celebrate the courage and imagination of the great Reformers, who assessed the church of their day, found it wanting in love and spirit, and set themselves to the task of redesigning the way they would live out their faith. Were it not for them, our church would not exist today, and the spiritual life of the world would be quite different. We praise you for their spiritual sensitivity and integrity, and for their willingness to pay any price, even their lives, for the reshaping of the community that bears the name of Christ. Help us to be worthy of their devotion and sacrifice. Teach us to become reformers in our own day, constantly praying about the forms and substance of our religious faith and pledging ourselves to the continuous and ongoing reformation of Christendom. Forgive us for the sins of our own church—for our self-preoccupation, our bureaucracy, our tendency to forget the care of the world and your little ones under the pressure of our own day-to-day decisions and the mistakes we make in judgment. Help us to be faithful as Jesus himself was faithful, holding always to the principle that it is your will that matters, not our own. Enable us to rise above the trendiness of our culture and the pettiness of our own inclinations to become the church you intended us to be. Show us the things that are wrong with our communion and give us the grace to mend them. Let the Christians of the world be led by Christ and not by fear or prejudice or personal desire. Grant that we may even lay down our lives as a sacrifice for others, willing the triumph of your kingdom over our inadequate imaginations and love and devotion. Let this be a day of renewal and recommitment for all of us, and a time of rejoicing and inspiration for the world at large, that the day may soon come when all the peoples of the earth shall look upon your glory and give praise to you for the majesty of your countenance. Through Christ our Lord and Savior. Amen.

Responsive Prayer

Leader: There are few days more important than this one, when we remember the importance of the continual reordering of our life and faith in the community of God.

People: **Show us, O God, the mistakes we have made as your people, and give us the courage to correct them without delay. Break our own stubborn wills and bend us to yours. Forgive us for the false idols we have worshiped and the wrong roads we have traveled. Renew our faith and help us to reconstruct the church in the image of Christ himself, humble and loving and subservient.**

Leader: May the blessings that flowed from the great reformation of the church in the days of Luther, Calvin, Zwingli, and Ignatius continue to flow in our time, and may we recommit ourselves to the honest, searching, and ever-reforming community of faith that was the goal of their lives and work.

People: **Send us forth today to pray and meditate on the life and future of our own church, and help us to pledge ourselves anew to its high and holy mission, in order that what is crooked may be made straight, what is dishonest may be made honest, and what is self-serving may be rejected for that which serves and honors you, so that all the world may be blessed through this dedicated fellowship of believers.**

All: **In the name of Christ our Lord. Amen.**

Suggested readings: Jeremiah 51:6-10; Psalm 82; Romans 4:13–5:5

ALL SAINTS DAY

Pastoral Prayer

TODAY, O God most high, we recognize all the blessed saints of your kingdom who have lived and gone before us into their heavenly home. Some of them, like Augustine, Luther, Wesley, and Mother Teresa, were famous. Most of them were not. Most of them were simple, ordinary folks like ourselves, people whose lives and labors were spent in quiet obscurity, without fanfare or special notice. Yet it was their faithfulness through the ages that kept the church alive and aided in the continuous preaching of your word. They gave their time and effort and often their meager resources to guarantee the ongoing of this community we now enjoy. They cared more for truth and honor than for the praises of the world. They loved Christ more than they loved themselves. They carved a way through the wilderness for us, and we are vastly indebted to them. Therefore we salute them and thank you for their lives, their witnesses, and their heritage. Help us to become worthy recipients of what they bequeathed to us, and to preserve the traditions and values dearest to them for those who will come after us in subsequent generations. Endow us with the same spirit of sacrifice that enabled them to fashion the church as they left it, and the imagination to represent Christ acceptably in the world. Let our lives too become monuments of trust and reliability to those who follow us, in order that your kingdom may be more fully known on earth. Through him who was the most blessed holy one of all, even Christ our Lord. Amen.

Responsive Prayer

Leader: We have always adored heroes, O God—heroes on the battlefield, heroes in the sports arena, heroes of civic virtue.

People: **We also adore the great heroes of faith—Abraham and Moses and Miriam and David and Ruth and Jesus and Mary and Peter and Mary Magdalene and Paul and Augustine and Luther and John and Charles Wesley and Albert Schweitzer and Mother Teresa.**

Leader: We thank you for all the souls that have gone before us in the faith, preparing a way for us in the wilderness of ideas and loyalties.

People: **They have made it easier for us to follow Christ in our time, and to seek your kingdom in a world that often pays little heed to spiritual values.**

Leader: Help us to become worthy of adoration ourselves, in order that future generations will not stumble for want of good examples and proper directions.

People: **Let the spirit that was in Christ Jesus our Lord inhabit our spirits as well, and direct our steps in the right paths, for your kingdom's sake, and that of all the saints. Amen.**

Suggested readings: Isaiah 52:7-10; Psalm 139:1-12; Philippians 1:1-11

Part Two

Civic Holidays

NEW YEAR'S EVE

Pastoral Prayer

WE HAVE COME to the final page of the book, O God, for the year that is past. It is now too late to change the plot or alter the fate of the characters. We can only offer the year to you and ask your blessings upon it. Accept all the good things that happened in it—the kind intentions, the generous acts, the signs of love—and forgive all the bad things—the selfishness, the wrangling, the ugly remarks, the hurtful behavior. We're sorry it wasn't a better year, and that we weren't better persons. We regret that we didn't follow Christ more faithfully. But we pray that we'll do better in the coming year, and that we'll be more responsible stewards of our relationship to you. Help us to spend more time being quiet and knowing that you are God. Help us to be more loving to our neighbors—and to our enemies. Help us to live more generously, sharing with others the many gifts you have entrusted to our care. Teach us to behave justly, to love mercy, and to walk humbly with you. Grant that the entire world may hear and understand the gospel in the coming year. Move the hearts of kings and presidents and parliaments to do your will. Bless all who have a role in peacemaking and peace-keeping throughout the globe. Let the spirit of our Christ become our spirit as well, and let the kingdoms of this world become his blessed kingdom of love and grace. For all of the ages are in your hands, O God, and you are the Lord, the most high God, forever and ever. Amen.

Unity Prayer

We celebrate the important beginnings and endings of our days, O God, because they deepen our consciousness and are a special part of our sacred journeys. Tonight we say good-bye to a year that is gone and prepare tomorrow to greet a whole new year. We would like to put our mistakes and failures behind us and face the future with a sense of release and optimism. Forgive us, we pray, for not having exploited these past months as much as we might have and for failing to fulfill all the resolutions we made a year ago. Help us, in the creative power of your forgiving love, to enter this new period of our lives with even greater hopes and expectations. Rekindle in us a sense of the mystery of our lives, and how they are ultimately involved with the global community and its welfare. Help us to rise above selfishness and become servants of Christ in a world that needs our love and healing. May every day of the coming year become an oblation of faithful service to you, O God, our maker and redeemer and Lord of all our years. Through Jesus Christ our Lord. Amen.

Suggested readings: Jonah 2; Psalm 143:5-8; Revelation 7:13-17

NEW YEAR'S DAY

Pastoral Prayer

THERE IS SOMETHING completely magical about gateways, O God. It is hardly any wonder that the ancients often regarded them as pathways to blessing. We too have a sense of their mystery and intrigue as we begin another year. We are leaving behind one chapter of our lives and opening another. We are now sensitive to the burdens we have borne in the previous year—all the illnesses, losses, failures, mistakes, broken promises, disrupted friendships, and unfulfilled dreams. But we are also keenly aware of the possibilities that lie before us—possibilities of new relationships, new growth, new work to do, new experiences of ourselves. We pray for the strength not to fail you in the coming year, or to fail ourselves; for when we fail you, we fail ourselves. Enable us to live passionately and courageously, deeply energized by the spirit of love and harmony that flow from you. Cast a spell over our lives that will make it easier for us to say the right words, do the right things, and construct the right future. Save us from any temptation to direct our own paths. Show us how to remake the world in your image and not in our own. Let our faith and our companionship with Christ give us stability when the seas around us are rough, and a sense of gratitude when they are not. Teach us to serve you in ways that will make our world more loving and more spiritual. And let us regard this particular gateway— the beginning of a new year—as the passageway to a closer and finer relationship with your spirit. Through Christ our Lord. Amen.

Responsive Prayer

Leader: We stand at the beginning of a new year, dear God.

People: **We are conscious of our mistakes and failures in the year that is gone.**

Leader: We repent of our sins and ask for your forgiveness in the name of Christ.

People: **Now we turn to the year that lies before us, and ask for your divine leadership in everything we do.**

Leader: Grant that this may be a year of spiritual advancement for all of us.

People: **And not for us only, but for the world in which we live.**

Leader: Help us to walk in humility of spirit and to seek your guidance at every step of the way.

People: **Teach us to pray and to listen, and to wait upon your Spirit.**

Leader: Let every day become a time for enjoying our relationship to you.

People: **Let every moment be a moment of communion, even though we may be unaware of it at the time.**

Leader: Bless the days that lie before us, that we may experience a deeper sense of your presence.

People: **And bless the lives that we offer you now, that they may be a blessing to others.**

All: **In the name of Christ our Lord. Amen.**

Suggested readings: Isaiah 42:9; Psalm 119:89-94; Revelation 21:1-7

MARTIN LUTHER KING, JR.'S BIRTHDAY

Pastoral Prayer

IT IS GIVEN to only a few people, O God, to rise above the crowds and become symbols of hope and passion to all of us. We thank you for these persons, from Moses and Christ to Gandhi and Martin Luther King, Jr., and for the way they remind us of your care and grace for all the little ones of the earth. We praise you today, on Dr. King's birthday, for the qualities that shaped his life: for a strong sense of justice, that regarded all souls as having importance in your eyes; for an unshakeable belief in love and gentleness, that would not permit him to turn to violence in order to achieve his dreams; for a commitment to sacrifice, that led him forward without regard for his own safety; and for an ultimate trust in you, that you would never abandon those who stand up for truth and righteousness in the world. We mourn what the world did to him—the pain and the degradation, and finally the death. But we celebrate the dream for which he stood, of a society where the lion and the lamb would lie down together, and the children of all races and backgrounds would mingle together in sweetness and harmony of spirit. Help us to be as committed to that dream as he was, to care as much about the poor and disenfranchised as he did, to be prepared to pay the price that he paid to insure its ultimate success. Teach us to love all men and women as our brothers and sisters, and to care as much about their welfare as we care about our own. And grant that we shall always have heroes whom we admire for their moral clarity, their unremitting courage, and their passion for righteousness, that your name and your way may be honored in all the world. Through Christ our Savior. Amen.

Responsive Prayer

Leader: We are grateful, O God, for those whose lives inspire our own.

People: **We pray that we may be more like them.**

Leader: Grant that we may aspire to more than a fleeting popularity and a temporary fame.

People: **Make us yearn for true greatness in our midst—for those who actually serve your kingdom with all their hearts and all their might.**

Leader: Help us to follow the real leaders and not the false leaders.

People: **Give us the grace to discern who the real leaders are, and to honor them while they are living.**

Leader: Let the spirit of Christ be in us all, to teach us truth and not error, and love and not hate.

People: **And grant that we may be ready, like your servant Martin Luther King, Jr., to pay any price in the service of your kingdom.**

All: **Through Jesus Christ, our Lord and Savior. Amen.**

Suggested readings: Exodus 32:7-14; Psalm 41:17-20; Romans 12:14-21; 13:1-2, 8-10

VALENTINE'S DAY

Pastoral Prayer

TODAY, O GOD, people all over the world have received greetings and gifts in the name of a saint who was noted for love. For some, it has been a trivial thing, something to prompt amusement; for others, it has been very serious, a time to speak from the heart. Help us always to be serious about love. We remember that the Bible says that you *are* love. It is your passionate selflessness, your disregard of status and reputation, your unremitting care for the least of all the people on earth, that identify you as the heart and soul of what love is and how it behaves in our midst. Without you, O God, all love would seem meaningless, a mere whimsical emotion that strikes us and then is gone. Forgive us, dear Father, for not loving enough, for not being more like you, for harboring hate and resentment in our hearts, for not seeking all the time and in every imaginative way we can to bring the world together in honest and loving harmony. Teach us to find love in our own souls each day, and to share that love with others as naturally as we share an interest in the weather or what we saw when we went to the mall. Bless our children with a sense of love, and make them loving in return. Let the love you have shown to us in Christ Jesus become our total way of life, in order that we may transcend all superficial, earthly kinds of love and glorify you forever. In the name of your eternal kingdom. Amen.

Responsive Prayer

Leader: The world is a practical place, O God, where people usually love those who love them and hate those who hate them.

People: **We would like to be impractical; we would like to follow Jesus' instructions to love even those who are our enemies, and those who abuse our love.**

Leader: We know it isn't easy, dear God; it goes against our very natures not to despise those who have despised us.

People: **Yet Jesus managed to love his enemies; he prayed for you to forgive the very people who crucified him. We would like to be like him.**

Leader: Send your Spirit upon us, O God, and change us into people who can no longer hate.

People: **Let the heavenly love that flowed through Jesus flow through us as his followers. Help us to change the world he wanted so much to change. Teach us to be Christ to our enemies.**

Leader: People may ridicule us and say we're naive; they may even persecute us for being like Jesus.

People: **The only thing that really matters to us, O God, is doing your will and following Jesus to the best of our ability.**

All: **For yours is the kingdom and the power and the glory, and that is all that really counts in the perspective of eternity. Amen.**

Suggested readings: Genesis 2:18-25; Psalm 112; 1 John 4:7-16

PRESIDENTS' DAY

Pastoral Prayer

MORE THAN ANY other deity that people may worship, O Lord, you are the God of history. Your revelation of yourself has always been intimately connected with personal development and the events that have shaped human relationships. We learned about you through your dealings with Moses and the formation of the people of Israel. Christianity was born in the cradle of the Middle East and its clash of cultures. The Middle Ages were shaped by wars between Christians and Muslims, and by the Crusades to recapture the Holy Land. Modern life was redefined by the Reformation and the quest for religious freedom. Our own country was born in that historical movement, and was developed by various groups of Christians who sought refuge here and then left their mark on our story. And our presidents, the famous men who presided over the helm of our national affairs, were all shaped in part by their belief in you and the destiny you imparted to our nation. Therefore we honor them, and in honoring them honor you, the Lord of our history. Give us a deep and abiding respect for the sound traditions that have established this country, O Lord, and make us ever cautious about departing from them. But give us with that respect an equally strong willingness to explore the wilderness that still lies before us, and to change our course whenever it is your will that we should do so. On the day when we remember our presidents, enable us to remember that we might never have existed as a country at all if you had not desired us to do so. Make us sensitive to our charge as a people to practice the love and grace and tolerance we have learned from you. Help us to live with our arms outstretched to the people of the world who are less fortunate than we are, and our hearts open to the poor and defenseless within our own boundaries. Show us how to live with a proper awareness of history and how it is made, and to create in our nation a living monument to your eternal kingdom. For you are God and we are your children, through Christ Jesus our Lord. Amen.

Unity Prayer

Teach us, O God, how to honor and respect our leaders. Make us humble and considerate citizens. But at the same time teach our leaders to be deeply thoughtful and responsive followers of your will. Make them compassionate toward the poor and helpless of the world, and give them a determination to serve the people they lead. We pray for our current president, _____, and ask that he/she may be shielded from danger, cradled in your love, and encouraged to do right. Make him/her sensitive to the most important demands on his/her time and energy, and let him/her serve you and his/her country with distinction and honor. Somewhere in this country, O God, there are several young boys and girls who will one day be elected to lead this great nation. Watch over them now, we pray, and provide them with the kinds of friendship, formation, and inner direction that will help them most when they become president. Grant to us who elect presidents the continuing insight and commitment to select candidates of great moral courage and wisdom, and the good will, when they have been elected, to support them in prayer and follow them in faithfulness and humility. Give us the grace to rise above politics and prejudice, and to honor you by the last full measure of citizenship. Through Jesus Christ our Lord. Amen.

Suggested readings: Exodus 35:4-21; Psalm 63; Romans 13:1-7; 14:7-9

ST. PATRICK'S DAY

Pastoral Prayer

ON THE DAY when we honor a famous saint named Patrick, O God, help us to honor at the same time the whole missionary endeavor of the Christian church. Let his legendary efforts to convert the land of Ireland, braving hardship and danger for the sake of Christ, inspire us to new considerations of the missionary task in our own age. It is so easy for us to become complacent, dear Father, living in comfort and worshiping in ways that are agreeable to us, and to forget that there are millions of people who have never heard about your love for them. Let the inspiration of Patrick, combined with his deep commitment to you and his unarguable heroism, remind us of how important it is to communicate our faith to others. We forget, when we live in the light, about all the people who live in shadows or darkness, and are still yearning for some hope to dawn in their lives. Make us sensitive to them, and inspire us to go to their aid. We have so much, and many of them have so little. Forgive us for our neglect of our commission from Christ to go into all the world with the story of the gospel, taking with it our means for healing the sick, establishing sound economies, and imparting a sense of global community. Remind us of the immensity of the love that has been shared with us, and enable us to share it with those who have known so little. Thus let the impact of St. Patrick's work among the Irish continue to influence our lives today, as ours may one day influence the lives of others. In the name of Christ, who came among us as a servant and rose from death to become our Lord. Amen.

Responsive Prayer

Leader: From age to age, God has always raised up certain people with the vision and courage to carry the gospel of Christ in places where he was little known.

People: **We are grateful for those who brought the gospel to our own forebears in the faith, thus paving the way for the joy we have experienced in Christ.**

Leader: We ask therefore, O God, for the continuance of your call in our own time, that we may be sensitive to the needs of others for the gospel and all its benefits.

People: **We pray that we ourselves may always be open to your special calling to us, and be ready to respond with our very lives and substance to the demands of the gospel.**

Leader: Help us to maintain an openness to the calling of our children, so that they are always aware of the priority of the gospel in our lives and theirs.

People: **In short, O God, let your name be always uppermost in our homes and in our lives outside the home, and let your Spirit lead to our complete dedication to the gospel.**

All: **Through Christ our Lord. Amen.**

Suggested readings: Deuteronomy 31:30–32:9; Job 42:1-6; Matthew 28:16-20

MOTHER'S DAY

Pastoral Prayer

YOU KNEW WHAT you were doing, O God, when you created mothers. You must have known what life would have been like without them—without their caring for us in our infancy, their worrying over us as teenagers, their continuing concern for us as we became adults. We would have been so poor, so lost, so lonely. The world would be unimaginable without mothers, or without those who have the loving and nurturing qualities of mothers. It would be all harsh and angular and businesslike. It would be an emotionless plain, an uncomfortable wilderness, an inhospitable and barren place. If all human beings are made in your image, then mothers must have been fashioned after your own warmth and forgiveness and unselfish caring. What a blessing they are in our lives, O God, and how we miss them when they are gone. We lift our prayers for all mothers today, wherever they are, in this country and around the world. We mourn with them for lost children, especially in war. Comfort them, O God, and help them to survive their losses. Be with those who have anguish of any kind—particularly those who can't be with their children as much as they would like because of employment or prison or military service. Let the mothering virtues of empathy and compassion become stronger and more prevalent in our world, until we become a global community and care as much about the children of others as we do about our own. Give our leaders mothering instincts. Let the songs and prayers and manners we learned at our mothers' knees become the songs and prayers and manners of our society. And grant that every mother in this place today will be given an extra measure of strength and patience and endurance. For yours are the grace and serenity and stamina we all need, through Jesus Christ our Lord. Amen.

Responsive Prayer

Leader: One of the most humanizing portraits in the world, O God, is the image of Jesus' mother and the suffering she endured for her son.

People: **Our own mothers have suffered too, O God, in giving birth to us and raising us from infancy.**

Leader: They have sacrificed time and energy for us.

People: **They have given themselves quietly and without fanfare because they loved us.**

Leader: Their love is a lot like yours.

People: **Teach us to love others as they have loved us, dear God. Give us the kind of patience and sympathy we have seen in them.**

Leader: Make us channels of your love and nurturing to others.

People: **Enable us to make life easier for others as they made it easier for us, and to honor them by imitating their goodness and sacrifice.**

All: **In the name of Christ, our Savior. Amen.**

Suggested readings: 1 Samuel 1:9-18; Psalm 1; Luke 1:39-49

MEMORIAL DAY

Pastoral Prayer

IF WE DID not remember the past, O God, our lives would not be worth living. Forgive us for ever thinking that our times are the only ones that matter, or that what has gone before us is not worthy of recollection. All life is fluid, and one age flows into another. We are inseparably linked to all who have preceded us and all who will come after us. And because most of human history has been marked by wars and conflicts of one kind or another, we praise you today for all those who have joined humanity's struggle in our behalf. Some are friends and relatives. Others are completely unknown to us except as ciphers or statistics. But they are all important. Their blood has been spilled, their lives given, for us who are alive today. We remember before you especially those who have been killed in recent combat—all the men and women who have died to protect our freedoms and the freedoms of others. We pray for their families, and what they have suffered. There will always be evil in the world, O God. Jesus said it would grow up like weeds in the grass, and that it is impossible to separate them. And as long as there is evil there will be war and death and destruction. Teach us sensitivity for all the dead, and for our own mortality. Help us to live as those who are indebted to others and as those who are going to die. Make us aware of the beauty and glory of life while we are able to enjoy it—of its sheer preciousness—and let us praise you for it. Reveal yourself to us in the thin line between life and death, this world and the next. We pray for all who suffer the lingering effects of battle—the many men and women who carry fragments of steel in their bodies, or walk with false limbs, or exist from day to day with mental or physical discomfort caused by the many forms of warfare. Comfort them, dear God, and give them peace in their hearts. Grant that all of us in the safety and comfort of this sanctuary may learn to pray daily for a world beyond the torment of war and battle, where the lion will lie down with the lamb and the bear will eat straw with the ox. For yours is the kingdom of ultimate peace and love, through Christ our Lord. Amen.

Responsive Prayer

Leader: There seems to be very little in our world today that is holy, O God; our media are filled with accounts of war and crime and violence.

People: **We live our lives with such busyness that we forget to have a sense of wonder, or to see you working behind the scenes in everything that happens.**

Leader: Help us to be more sensitive, dear God; teach us to celebrate your presence in all things.

People: **Show us how to be more like little children, who take delight in the small things and realize how miraculous they are.**

Leader: Enable us to see you even in the unpleasantness of war and privation, in the struggles that engulf our lives and command all our energies.

People: **For you are literally the God of everything, of the darkness as well as the light, of death as well as life, and being able to see you in such contradictions is part of the faith we are trying to live.**

All: **Therefore we praise you, O God, and beseech you to live among us as our Lord, a very present help in time of trouble. Amen.**

Suggested readings: Joshua 23:1-11; Psalm 107:1-9; Revelation 21:1-7

FATHER'S DAY

Pastoral Prayer

FATHER: IT IS THE NAME, O God, that Jesus taught his followers to call you. It is so different from King of Kings, Lord Almighty, and all the other names by which you were known in the past. It breathes a sense of care, of personal recognition, of relationship. It reminds us of your tender interest in everything about us—our health, our happiness, our behavior, our fulfillment as persons. We thank you, dear God, for this revelation about you. And we thank you for the way it honors our earthly fathers as well. Earthly fathers aren't as perfect as you; sometimes they ignore us or abuse us or behave shamelessly. But we are grateful for them, and acknowledge that they could never be completely like you. Bless all the fathers who are here today, we pray, and grant them a sense of their importance in our lives and the lives of their children. Let them recognize the mystery in which we all live—a mystery in which we are bound up with you and with one another—and let it inspire them to live joyfully and responsibly before you. We pray for fathers around the world, and ask that they may be imbued with your spirit to be sensitive to all those depending on them. Teach us to get up every day with a feeling of confidence because we are living in our Father's world, and to know that our Father really cares for us, whatever we are saying or doing. For you are truly our heavenly Parent and we are your children forever and ever. Amen.

Responsive Prayer

Leader: It is very special, O God, for us to be able to call you "Father."

People: **Somehow it makes you seem closer and more intimately involved in our lives.**

Leader: We pray that we may live in daily appreciation of your closeness and involvement.

People: **Teach us to remember that we are never alone, because you are always with us and ready to help us.**

Leader: Remind us of your presence in such a way that we feel stronger and better able to deal with the tasks of our daily existence.

People: **Help us to live with the confidence of those who know that their Father is always there to guide and protect them.**

Leader: Grant that it may make us more thoughtful of others, and ready to share your love and benefits with them.

People: **For your fatherly love is without measure, and there is more than enough for all the people in the world.**

All: **Amen.**

Suggested readings: Genesis 22:1-14; Psalm 8; Luke 15:11-24; Ephesians 6:1-4

INDEPENDENCE DAY

Pastoral Prayer

WE LOVE OUR country, O God, with its "fruited plains," its "purple mountains' majesty," its red-white-and-blue freshness among the nations, its no-mountain-too-high, no river-too-wide attitude, its brassy, congested cities and its lazy, familiar little country towns, its church spires and hospitals, its audacious skyscrapers and sprawling airports, its clanging mills and computerized technological systems, its razzmatazz musicals and its great libraries, its simple folks and its scholars, its august holiness and its peppery secularity. We treasure its storied past, with characters like George and Martha Washington and Davy Crockett and Mark Twain and Teddy Roosevelt and Susan B. Anthony and Will Rogers and Babe Ruth and Annie Oakley and Louis "Satchmo" Armstrong. We revere its strength and complexity in the world today, with its global economic empires, its vast medical systems, its formidable military power, its great research engines, and its incredible think tanks and universities. But we pray for its soul, dear God, that you will guard it against complacency and self-satisfaction, against pride and over-confidence, against disregard for the plight of others, and against indifference to the evil within it. Nurture and care for the good that is in our nation, and defend that good against all change and deterioration. Give strength of heart and mind and soul to our president, our Congress, and all other officers of our government. Remind them daily of their fealty to you and the spirit of righteousness. And grant, dear God, that our national aim for all the years to come will be to channel your gifts of love and support to all the peoples of the world, in order that the kingdoms of this world may one day become the kingdom of our Christ. For his name's sake. Amen.

Responsive Prayer

Leader: Something lifts our hearts on the Fourth of July, O God.

People: **We love a parade, and fireworks, and waving flags, and the enthusiasm of the crowds.**

Leader: We also love the reminder of who we are as a nation, and what our forefathers and mothers believed.

People: **Teach us to be reverent of the past in order that we may live nobly in the present.**

Leader: Make us mindful of the sacrifices of others that allow us to celebrate our freedom and independence today.

People: **And let us live with a sense of spiritual responsibility in a world that is hungry for the things we enjoy about our own country.**

Leader: Show us how to be channels of blessing to the rest of the world's population.

People: **Let the love and ministry of Christ flow through us to everyone on this globe.**

All: **For your gifts are for all of us, and your kingdom is forever. Amen.**

Suggested readings: Genesis 1:9-19; Psalm 111; 1 Corinthians 2

LABOR DAY

Pastoral Prayer

BEFORE ANYTHING WAS, O God, you were a worker, a maker, a creator. You shaped the earth from the void, and the heavens around it as a velvet pillow to display it. You made the jungles and the deserts, the mountains and the valleys, the lands and the seas. You fashioned the birds and the animals, the creatures in the ocean, and the man and woman who were our progenitors. It isn't any wonder that we are called to work as well, and to fill the world with our produce, our art, and our handiwork. We praise you today for the ability to work—to apply ourselves with diligence and constancy, to bring about beauty and order on the earth, to provide for ourselves and others, to imitate your holy ways by revering that which is made by human hands and ingenuity. We pray for all workers throughout the globe—those who design and those who execute; those who perform on the stage and those who sell and take the tickets; those who make vast sums of money and those who labor for almost nothing; those who invent and those who imitate; those who begin and those who sustain; those who spend an hour in the vineyards and those who work throughout the day. Give us a hearty respect for all kinds of work and the people who do it. Help us to improve the conditions of those who work the hardest and receive the least from their labors. And let us all be instructed by the words of our Savior, who said, "Do not work for the food that perishes, but for the food that endures for eternal life." Teach us to work as hard at our spiritual lives as we do at our physical well-being, and to set aside time for communing with you when our other work is done. That way we shall rejoice in all of life, and be glad for the gift of each day and the work that is accomplished in it. For yours is the kingdom that is eternal in the heavens, and we are your children through Jesus Christ our Lord. Amen.

Responsive Prayer

Leader: You have reminded us, dear God, that there is an integral relationship between faith and works, between what we believe and what we do.

People: **Help us to be concerned, therefore, about what we do and how we go about it. Make us sensitive to the way in which we live in the earth, and how we make our living and handle our finances, and what we say to others by the way we behave.**

Leader: Give us your grace to guide us in all the decisions of our lives and the way we treat others around us.

People: **Let us live carefully each day, measuring our responses to all events, and shape our existences with love and thoughtfulness. Show us how to make the most of our possibilities, and teach us to sing and dance with joy for the outcome of all our efforts.**

Leader: Make us truly thankful for the opportunity to work and create, to live in the company of others, and to forge relationships that will last a lifetime.

People: **And give us, above all, an appreciation for the work of Christ in our behalf, who has died on the Cross to save us from our sin and lives forever as our elder brother in the Spirit.**

All: **For we pray in his name, and for the sake of his kingdom. Amen.**

Suggested readings: Genesis 2:4-9, 15-17; Psalm 112:1-9; John 6:25-35

HALLOWEEN

Pastoral Prayer

ON THE EVE of All Saints Day, O God, we remember a world of spirits and demons within which the saints have always labored. We send our children from door to door in costumes of fun and fantasy, receiving the alms and good will of friends and neighbors, and tell stories of ghosts and goblins and witches and devils. Even though it is all in pretense and play, help us to remember the serious plight of those who are enmeshed in evil, and whose lives are being plundered by drugs and crime and abusive human situations. Use this occasion to remind us of the way the worlds of good and evil spirits are interwoven, and the ease with which we can all become subjected to wicked passions and overbearing temptations. Help us to pledge anew our fealty to Christ and the angels, and to see more clearly the way we should live and be in the real world where we contend for an eternal prize. Make us sensitive to the needs and requirements of others, and help us to respond to them generously and without stint. Bless our children with a sense of what is right and wrong, and what is pleasing to you and what is displeasing. Secure our hearts and minds with memories of Jesus and his resistance of the devil. And let his crucifixion and resurrection so command our imaginations that we shall always be ready to die for our faith in order to live in new life with him. For his name's sake. Amen.

Responsive Prayer

Leader: From the beginning of his ministry, O God, Jesus contended with the evil spirits.

People: **Teach us to contend as well, and not to surrender to the easiest path that opens before us. Make us sensitive to the issues that govern our lives, and help us to make the decisions that will bind us closer to you.**

Leader: Help us to do justly, to love mercy, and to walk humbly with you.

People: **Enable us to resist temptations, to love others, to forgive our enemies, and to reflect honorably upon our Lord and Savior, Jesus Christ.**

Leader: Enable us at all times to call upon your Holy Spirit to strengthen and sustain us.

People: **And guide us faithfully along our spiritual journeys.**

All: **For the world is a deceptive place, and we should move through it wisely and carefully. In Jesus' name. Amen.**

Suggested readings: Amos 6:1-7; Isaiah 42:10-20; Acts 14:8-18

VETERANS DAY

Pastoral Prayer

THERE HAVE ALWAYS been wars, dear God, because there have always been problems between human beings. As long as there has been history, battle lines have been drawn and people have fought with one another. We wish it were not so, and that we human beings had the kind of love and insight that would prevent war. But, as it is so and we don't have that kind of love and insight, we offer our prayers for all those who have volunteered or been conscripted to fight their countries' wars. We thank you for their courage and often their heroism as they have faced the enemy in battle. We praise their selfless acts in behalf of fellow soldiers. We extol their wisdom gathered from the battlefield, and commend their eternal souls to your loving and forgiving care. We remember especially all who presently serve in the armed forces of this and other countries, and pray for their continued safety and welfare. As they encounter danger, give them the insight to understand life and death, and enable them to be at peace with you and with themselves. Bless the families of all who serve in the armed forces, and let your Holy Spirit rest upon them like a mantle to preserve them from anxiety and harm. Grant to each and every one of us a reminder of the way life itself is a struggle between good and evil, and prepare us to defend the good and not succumb to the evil we encounter. For yours is the kingdom and the power and the glory forever. Amen.

Responsive Prayer

Leader: We remember today, O God, all those who have served under the colors of their countries.

People: **We commend them to you for their bravery, their patriotism, and their honor.**

Leader: Grant that those who serve today may be kept in your everlasting love and protection.

People: **Give comfort and encouragement to their families.**

Leader: We pray for the day when there will be peace on earth and the kingdoms of this world will have become the kingdoms of our Christ.

People: **Hasten that day, O God, and help us to live in that hope. Imbue us with your spirit of love and forgiveness, in order that we may understand the nature of Christ's kingdom.**

Leader: Hear our prayers for our enemies in the world, that they may be converted to Christ's will for the nations and join us in a better world community.

People: **Let your holy will prevail among all people, and your name be exalted forever.**

All: **Amen.**

Suggested readings: Isaiah 45:22-25; Psalm 20; Matthew 13:24-30

THANKSGIVING

Pastoral Prayer

WE ARE REMINDED by one of our poetic saints,[1] O God, that gratefulness is the heart and center of all prayer. Not faithfulness, not sacrifice, not service, but gratefulness. Help us therefore to be truly grateful for all your gifts to us—for an incomparably beautiful world filled with trees and flowers and mountains and rivers and oceans; for our bodies that are so intricately and incredibly made, with hearts and brains and stomachs and nerves and veins, all fitted around frameworks of bone and sinew that make us mobile and functional; for our networks of family and friends, who sustain us with love and joy and companionship, so that we are much more than we could ever be alone; for all the churches and synagogues and mosques of the world, where people retreat to contemplate you in the various ways they know you; for the wonders of technology, medicine, and transportation that sustain and enrich our lives today; and for the gospel of Jesus Christ, that reminds us of your mercy and forgiveness and your love and compassion for us, even when we fail to be thoughtful and sensitive and grateful. Our imaginations are too small, dear God, to understand how wonderfully connected everything is, and how we are part of a divine fabric that comprises all creation and binds us to every living

---

1. Brother David Steindl-Rast, *Gratefulness: The Heart of Prayer* (New York: Paulist Press, 1984).

thing in the universe. We are grateful that you love and provide for us in spite of our vast limitations, and that you are bringing us at last into the full peace and harmony of your everlasting kingdom. As we celebrate today an event that occurred centuries ago, when the first pilgrims in this country set aside a time to honor you for sustaining them in the new world, help us to look forward as well to the final gathering of all your saints into a heavenly rest, where all life centers on you and your Son Jesus and we shall be caught up in eternal gratitude. Amen.

Unity Prayer

We are thankful today for many things, O God: for our families and friends, our comfortable homes, the education provided for us, the work we are allowed to do, the convenience of food and goods, the ease of transportation, the blessing of an advanced medical system, the safety of our surroundings, and the comfort of our faith in all difficult and trying situations. Forgive us, we pray, for the days when we forget to be grateful, and go on our way as if all these things were our natural right and had not come about by the sensitivity and effort and sacrifice of others. We pray for all those around this globe who do not have as much as we for which to be thankful—those who are hungry or poor; those who lack medical care; those who have AIDS or other terrible diseases; those who are spending Thanksgiving in hospitals or prisons or far away from their families; and those who are not part of the communion of Christ and his church. Help us, out of our bounty, to learn to share what we have with them and to make this world more like your kingdom of love and light. Through Jesus our Lord. Amen.

Suggested readings: Proverbs 3:4-18; Isaiah 60:1-5; 1 Thessalonians 4

Part Three

Special Days
in the Congregation

BAPTISMAL SERVICE

Pastoral Prayer

WE REMEMBER, O God, how Jesus was baptized and led into the wilderness by your Spirit at the beginning of his ministry. In a way, we are at such a beginning now for these children being baptized in our midst. Their lives will be different because they have been baptized. Their parents and loved ones will regard them differently. And as they learn more and more through the years about the significance of this rite and its importance in their development as followers of Jesus, they will realize that their whole lives have been marked by what we are doing here today. We thank you for their young souls, and for the dedication of their parents in bringing them to be set aside as your future servants. Bless them with your presence, we pray, from this day forth. Watch over them in their play, in their education, in their relationships, and in the work they will do. Help us to teach them the kinds of truths that will enable them to live confidently and gracefully, and to discover the special truths that only they can find for themselves. Make their hearts generous and happy, and incline them to a moral and compassionate existence. Give their parents the wisdom to deal with them fairly and thoughtfully, with the kind of loving discipline that will provide boundaries but not walls. And grant that this community of believers may always encourage them to walk humbly and hopefully in the path of Christ, so that they become a blessing to their parents, their friends, and the world beyond. For yours are the kingdom and the power and the glory forever. Amen.

Unity Prayer

We invoke your Spirit on these children, dear God, and ask that they may be kept forever in your love and care. Help them to grow in stature and in favor with you and their parents and the entire community. Grant that we shall provide the kinds of examples and inspiration that will guide and encourage them in their Christian development. Give wisdom and grace especially to their parents and teachers, that they may instruct them in joy and discipline them in love. Make us all mindful of our own baptisms, and of the importance of being marked for the service of Christ. May the spirit and understanding of this moment continue in all our lives and not be lost in the busyness of our daily affairs. And may the angels in heaven rejoice with us this day at your gift of baptism. For we ask it in the name of your Son, our Lord, Jesus Christ. Amen.

Suggested readings: Genesis 32:22-31; Psalm 67; Acts 8:26-39

BIBLE PRESENTATION TO CHILDREN SUNDAY

Pastoral Prayer

WE ARE NOT FANATICS about the Bible, O God, and do not use it to make preposterous arguments or to prove things that are not so. But we revere it as the most important book in the history of the world because it contains so many testimonies to your grace and your interaction with people who have known and worshiped you. Without it, we would not know you as we do. Without it, there would be no church, no Christian understanding of the world, no compelling evidence of how we should lead our lives. Therefore we praise you for this book and what it has meant in the lives of millions of people, and we invoke your sacred blessing on the copies of it we present now to these children of our congregation. Help them to read it under the guidance of your Holy Spirit, in order that their lives may be touched by the grace and understanding to which it testifies. Let them encounter in it the great stories of our collective past, and thus come to a life-changing meeting with you and with your Son, whose sayings and actions contribute so much to its final substance. Teach them to linger over its essential witness, in order that they may be shaped by that witness into strong and compassionate adults, capable of existing wisely and confidently in a world of sometimes difficult and intransigent realities. And may the power of your Spirit, which we meet so powerfully and inevitably within the pages of this book, keep them and lead them this day and throughout their years on earth. In the name of the Father, Son, and Holy Spirit. Amen.

Responsive Prayer

Leader: This is a wonderful book, dear God, and it is an important moment when a congregation presents it to its children.

Children: **We thank you, O God, for the stories and teachings of this book, and we pray that we may read and understand them with the help of your Holy Spirit.**

Leader: Let the witness of these pages, written so long ago, come alive for us today, and shape and direct our lives.

Everyone (including children): **Grant that we may honor you by our constant study of this book, and by learning to live by the example and instructions of Christ, so clearly told within these pages.**

Leader: Help us to give this book a place of honor in our homes and in our daily lives, that your name may be glorified.

Everyone (including children): **May we learn to do justly, to love mercy, and to walk humbly with you. Through Jesus Christ our Lord. Amen.**

Suggested readings: 2 Chronicles 34:29-33; Psalm 19:7-11; 2 Timothy 3:10-17

SENDING OUT MISSION TEAMS

Pastoral Prayer

AT THE HEART OF everything we know about our Savior, O God, is the fact that he left the comfort of his life with you to become a slave and a servant of all. For that reason, we understand that the highest and most honorable thing we can do with our lives is to follow him in service and love. We pray for your blessing on these friends and loved ones of ours being commissioned today to go into (the community/another part of the world) with their gifts and abilities to improve the lives and situations of others. May they go in health and strength, and in the joy of knowing that their service is not only to other persons but to you. Anoint them with compassion, insight, and courage to do the things they must do. Reveal the thoughts they should think and the actions they should undertake. Let them feel led in every way to comfort, encourage, and strengthen others by sharing both their love and their talents. And grant, in the end, that this church may be a stronger and better community because of their going on this heavenly mission. Let the spirit of Christ be and abide in our hearts forever, and may we always exalt you as the Lord of our lives, supremely present in everything we do. Amen.

Responsive Prayer

Leader: We were not saved, O Lord, for ourselves alone, but for the world you created and have always loved.

People: **Therefore we invoke your blessing on these our friends and loved ones who have volunteered to go in service to others.**

Leader: We pray for them that they may go in health and strength, and that they may find great rewards of the Spirit through what they will be doing.

People: **Let them prove a valuable help to those to whom they go, and an inspiration to us as well.**

Leader: Equip them with your wisdom and insights, that they may accomplish all that you will them to do.

People: **Grant that they may exalt the name of Christ by going as his** servants, and thus achieve even more by their work than will meet the eye.

All: **Let those who go to bless be blessed in return, and let the spirit of our Lord rest upon them in all they do. For his name's sake. Amen.**

Suggested readings: 1 Samuel 3; Psalm 65; Acts 13:1-3

STEWARDSHIP SUNDAY

Pastoral Prayer

THE CATTLE ON A thousand hills are yours, O God, and all the oil and corn in the world. How can we presume to own anything? Everything we have is a trust from you. Therefore we ask, on this stewardship Sunday, for sensitivity to your owner-ship. Forgive us for having ever claimed anything for our own, for having said, "This house is mine" or "This bank account belongs to me." It is your grace that has blessed us with homes and families and cars and food and clothing and computers and everything. Teach us, then, to say, not "This is ours" but "This is yours, O Lord, what do you wish to be done with it?" And in the mood of that, enable us to see how much we should be sharing with the world. Remind us of little children who are starving because they don't have enough food, and whole tribes that are dying of AIDS, and millions of people who will lie down in darkness tonight because they have never heard the good news of the gospel. Open our eyes to the hunger and poverty in our own community—to the hundreds of people who must choose between buying medicine and buying food, and hundreds of others who ration their heat and don't ever have any air-conditioning in the summer. We are here to serve you, O God, by serving them. Don't let us be presumptuous enough to think that we can be successful human beings by continuing to feed our own addictions and desires without caring for others. Show us the sheer joy of sharing. Let the glory of Christ's spirit come upon us and make our hearts full and generous. Help us to be mature followers of Jesus and not hollow people who pretend to live in your Spirit. Then we shall praise you with true enthusiasm and wonder at our own transformations. For you are the Maker and Sustainer of all, the loving Parent who wants to be proud of us and the decisions we make. Through Jesus Christ our Lord. Amen.

Responsive Prayer

Leader: This is an important day in the life of our church.

People: **It is an important day in our lives as individuals, for it is an occasion when we measure our faithfulness to Christ.**

Leader: Jesus said there are many who call him "Lord, Lord," but do not do his will.

People: **We would like to be true followers of Jesus, and not mere nominal Christians who don't really follow him at all.**

Leader: We know that the real blessings of God are for those who are truly committed to him and his kingdom.

People: **Therefore we want to offer him our hearts and minds and souls in all their fullness, and follow him with all we have.**

Leader: If we do that, he has promised to bless us, and to make us prosper in all the ways that matter.

All: **The Lord is our shepherd, and he shall lead us into the paths of righteousness for his name's sake, and restore our souls all the days of our lives. It is an honor to be his children, and to be faithful to him forever. Amen.**

Suggested readings: Job 9:1-12; Psalm 49; Luke 21:1-4

SEPTEMBER 11

Pastoral Prayer

THE PAIN IS STILL there, O God, especially for those who lost loved ones on that awful day. And the shock is still there, for all of us. We had begun to think of ourselves as invulnerable, a nation almost beyond attack. And then they came—men who hated us for our well-being, our prosperity, and the arrogance they perceived to accompany it. Men who were desperate to make us hear and understand that we are not invulnerable, and that their people have long suffered under the policies of our government. Forgive us that we had not heard before, and that when we did hear it made us hate them, so that once again we didn't hear. Our globe is growing smaller and smaller, dear God, so that what any of us do affects all the others. Help us to be more sensitive than we have been in the past. Let the spirit of Christ shine in our hearts, so that we may choose ways that are loving and forgiving and unselfish. We do not condone the evil done by others; but help us that we may not compound the evil by despising those who do it. Show us new ways for new times. Help us to have compassion for all your little ones around the globe. Make us emissaries of hope and healing. Let our hearts recover from their own wounds, and then let us tend the wounds of others. Grant to our world a new vision of what we can be as children of God, and let that vision affect everything we do. For it is really your kingdom that we care about, not our own, and we praise you through Christ our Lord. Amen.

Responsive Prayer

Leader: Some days live on in infamy long after they are past.

People: **September 11 is one of those days, O God. None of us who were alive will ever forget it.**

Leader: It was a horrible time, but it brought us close together and close to you.

People: **We truly felt your presence then, O God. We couldn't have lived through the pain without you.**

Leader: Wouldn't it be wonderful, dear God, if we could feel your presence that way all the time, without the terrible thing that prompted it?

People: **We want to live that close to you, our Father, for you are our rock and our salvation, a very present help in times of trouble.**

Leader: Teach us to be receptive to your Spirit at any time, and under all conditions.

People: **Make us sensitive to you in the ticking of a clock, the beauty of a flower, the embrace of a friend. Let everything mediate your loving presence to us, and cause us to rejoice in every moment.**

Leader: For you are our God and we are your people, today and every day, for the rest of our lives.

People: **Hallelujah and amen, for the rest of our lives. Amen.**

Suggested readings: Jeremiah 50:4-7; Isaiah 42:18-25; Luke 6:37-49

WORLD COMMUNION SUNDAY

Pastoral Prayer

WHEN YOU MADE THE world, O God, it was one. We the inhabitants divided it into parts and called them our own. We developed different languages and ways of expressing ourselves. We made many religions and originated many kinds of culture. And now we pay a price for it every day that we live, and make you pay a price for it too. But Christ has died that we might be one again, and that we might all desire your kingdom above our own. And because of Christ, there are disciples of his in every nation on earth, in every language and every culture. We honor that today, and pray for his preeminence in all our lives and communities. We exalt him in order that our lives may once again become one in you, and ask that your Holy Spirit may bind us together in prayer and worship wherever followers call upon your name. Let love and fellowship prevail among us, O God, transforming the world around us. May

Christ preside over every table where Christians gather, and may our hymns and songs redound to your glory, for your mercy's sake. Amen.

Responsive Prayer

Leader: It is Christ himself who serves us at his table, saying, "Take, eat, this is my body."

People: **We join together with Christians everywhere, O God, drawn by the gift of Christ's life in our behalf.**

Leader: Banish our sin, and help us to come forgiving one another.

People: **May the blood of Christ atone for all our sins and make us brothers and sisters with other Christians around the world.**

Leader: Let Christ be glorified in our spirit of unity.

People: **Grant that our oneness with other worshipers may lead to greater opportunities for the gospel, and that the kingdoms of this earth may soon become the kingdom of our Christ.**

All: **We pray in his name. Amen.**

Suggested readings: Exodus 12:21-27; Psalm 24; 1 Corinthians 11:23-29

CHRISTIAN EDUCATION SUNDAY

Pastoral Prayer

AFTER JESUS CALLED HIS disciples, O God, they followed him for years to learn from him. This accuses us. It means that giving our hearts to Jesus isn't enough—that it is also important to keep learning about him. We thank you that, with modern Christian education, it is so possible for us to do this. We praise you for all the great educators who have devised and developed such a system, and for all the authors whose writings have helped provide the content for it. We thank you for the many people who volunteer to become educators in their local churches, and pray for your Spirit to continue to motivate and inhabit them. Help us always to take Christian learning seriously, and to understand how completely it underwrites our other programs and our intentions as a church. We ask for your guidance in knowing how to teach people about Jesus and his kingdom. Save us from the error of merely repeating what others have said or done in the past. Make us open to new possibilities, new curricula, new materials, new media, new understandings, so that we may truly live in the freedom and inspiration of your Spirit. Grant that what we teach and how we do it may help people, especially the young, to become so excited about Jesus and his ministry that they themselves will want to teach, and will help to supply the church's continual need for new witnesses to the old, old story. To that end, O God, let your holy presence become a guide and standard for everything we do in life, especially in this church. Through Jesus our Lord. Amen.

Responsive Prayer

Leader: Today, O God, we focus on Christian education and its role in our fellowship.

People: **We honor great teachers we have had, who have helped make the gospel more relevant to us and have opened our eyes to its implications for everything we do.**

Leader: Bless those teachers, O God, and continue to give them wisdom and insight to share with others.

People: **We thank you for books and libraries, for audio and video tapes, and for all the other aids that have helped us understand your Word and its meanings for our lives.**

Leader: Help us always to be sensitive, dear God, to the needs of others who have not understood the meaning of Christ and his kingdom for their lives, and to continue trying to shine the light of the gospel into the darkness of their situations.

People: **Grant that we may all accept the responsibility of the old directive, "each one teach one," so that we shall be involved in fulfilling Christ's admonition to go into all the world and teach every creature. Let the mantle of your Spirit be upon us to inspire and encourage us.**

All: **For you, O God, are the most important dimension of our lives,** and we want to honor you by making that clear. Through Jesus Christ our Lord. Amen.

Suggested readings: 1 Kings 8:1-11; Psalm 93; Matthew 4:23–5:11

CHOIR AND MUSIC SUNDAY

Pastoral Prayer

TODAY, O GOD, we thank you for music, which is one of the most integral and important factors in our lives. We cannot imagine our history without music—without the chanting of the monks, the plainsong of the cathedrals, the haunting spirituals of the Negro slaves, the blues that grew out of them, jazz, and rock-and-roll and rap, without Bach and Handel and Mozart and Beethoven and Chopin and Rachmaninoff and Sondheim, without harps and lutes and trumpets and drums and bands and orchestras and organists and pianists and choirs and soloists. Before the great credos of the church were spoken, they were sung, and before any of us became theologians or preachers, we intoned the great hymns of the faith. Music is one of your greatest gifts, O God, and it isn't any wonder that the angels in heaven adore you in song. We thank you for its impact on our lives—for the way it has lifted our spirits when we were low or filled us with ardor when we were apathetic or lulled us into serenity when we were angry or illuminated our paths when we were walking in darkness. We are grateful for what we have learned about Christ through hymns, for how we have felt moved to follow him because of them, and for how we have been encouraged to keep following him by the songs we have heard and known. We ask your special blessing on every person in this congregation who has helped enrich our lives and our community by his or her contribution to our music—the minister of music, the organist, the pianists and other instrumentalists, the bell-ringers, the directors of various choirs, and all the people who form those choirs. They have strengthened and encouraged our faith by setting it to music and filling our hearts with music, and we honor them for this and all their faithfulness. Through Jesus Christ our Lord. Amen.

Responsive Prayer

Leader: It would be hard for us to exist as a church, O God, without music.

People: **We like to sing our faith, and to express our love to you in song.**

Leader: We cannot imagine life without song, or faith without the music that expresses it.

People: **The great hymns and choruses of the faith have strengthened us when we were weak and helped us move on when we were immobilized.**

Leader: They have helped us bury our dead, teach our children, carry our heaviest loads, and draw nearer to you when we were far away.

People: **We thank you, O God, for our great musical traditions, and pray for the present generation of composers and writers, that they may continue contributing to the greatness of the church through music.**

Leader: We ask your blessings on all who have enriched the musical programs of this church, and who will continue to do so in the future.

People: **And we pray that our hearts will go on being moved by the great music of the faith, so that we may follow Christ with joy and enthusiasm.**

All: **For yours are the kingdom and the power and the glory forever. Amen.**

Suggested readings: Exodus 15:1-3, 20-21; Psalm 150; Revelation 19:1-10

HOMECOMING SUNDAY

Pastoral Prayer

IT IS ALWAYS GOOD to go home, O God. We are grateful that our final home is in you, for that is where our hearts are. But in the meantime it is wonderful to return to our earthly roots, and to celebrate the sense of joy and familiarity we feel when we go there. We praise you for the folks at home, and we praise you for those who move away, live their lives creatively in other places, and then come home to be a part of us again. It reminds us that the whole earth is yours, and that wherever we go, we are still part of a larger family. We thank you for the things about home that remain comfortable to us—the good people we knew, the memories that are rekindled when we return, the places where we once walked and sat and studied, the stores where we shopped, the church where they sing the old songs, pray real prayers, and declare the gospel the way they always did. And we thank you for what those returning bring to us at home—a sense of freshness, a reminder that there is a world out there beyond the one we know, a witness to the power of the church and the congregation to draw them back, and a testimony to the way the gospel continues to go out from this place to the farthest corners of the earth. Help us to remember the old times, but help us to feel something new as well—an assurance that life goes on and is good, and the knowledge that our fellowship in you can never be broken, regardless of how far we roam or what we do. Let the spirit of Christ reign in our hearts today, and make us glad together. And let your name be glorified in the renewal we experience. For you are our God, and we have never forgotten it! Amen.

Responsive Prayer

Leader: Surely, dear God, there isn't anybody who doesn't enjoy a homecoming!

People: **All the people we see, the great singing, the heightened sense of your presence, the delicious food . . .**

Leader: We praise you, Lord, for this opportunity, and for the joy of being together this way.

People: **We ask your special blessing on everybody who is here, and we pray for all of those who couldn't be here.**

Leader: Grant that this day may strengthen our hearts and remain in our minds for a long time.

People: **And let your Holy Spirit fall upon us, to rekindle our experience of Christ and renew our dedication to him.**

Leader: For we are all your children and we want to do your will.

People: **We pray this in the name of Jesus our Lord, to whom be glory and honor, power and dominion, forever and ever. Amen.**

Suggested readings: Genesis 32:9-21; 33:1-11; Psalm 133; Acts 2:1-11

CONFIRMATION SUNDAY

Pastoral Prayer

THERE IS NO GREATER satisfaction, O God, than the satisfaction you give us in our children. And there is no greater blessing that comes to people of faith than to see their offspring following in the path of their faith and learning to view the world from their perspective. Therefore we thank you for this occasion, and for these young men and women who appear before us today, having completed their course of study and development, to have their understandings of God and Christian theology confirmed by the church. We pray for them to realize how important this step is in their development as citizens of God's kingdom, and that it will not be the end, but only the beginning, of their pilgrimage in the faith. Help them understand that they have been provided with only the barest outlines of a map, and that it is now their lifelong business, as it is ours, to explore the vast and fascinating territories within that map. Grant that their arriving at this point today may remind us all of the importance of our continued journeying in the mysteries of faith, and call us once again to the alluring, wonderful road of spiritual discovery. You have blessed us, O God, with the ministry and teachings of Christ, with the long history of the church and its doctrines, and with teachers and ministers who have labored through the years to make the way of understanding easier for us. Now help us, each one, to accept the responsibility of going forward, of using what has been given to us as stepping stones toward our own new explorations and discoveries, that Christ, who is not a destination but a way, may be glorified in our growth and excitement. To that end, we celebrate the arrival of these young people at this milestone in their journey, and, having greeted them here, set off together with them on the next segment of our general travels in the faith. Through Christ, who always goes before us and bids us to follow. Amen.

Responsive Prayer

Leader: These lovely young people, O God, have worked hard to master the essential teachings of the Christian faith. They stand here now as pilgrims on the road to fuller understanding.

Children: **We thank you, O God, for what we have learned. We pray that it may be only the beginning, and that we shall now go forward to learn much more about what it means to live in Christ, our Lord.**

Leader: Grant that their discoveries may prove so rewarding that they shall be eager to continue learning and growing.

Children: **We ask that what we have learned in our minds may be felt in our hearts, and that our experiences as children of the heavenly kingdom will be rich and meaningful.**

Leader: Let the parents of these young people and other adults in their lives always set good examples before them of the life in Christ and the way we are to think and live as servants of the Most High.

Adults: **Make us aware of our shortcomings as leaders of the young, and help us to be more worthy of our leadership roles. We too are only children in the heavenly kingdom, and our knowledge is often imperfect. Teach us to walk more consistently with Christ and to embody his teachings in our daily affairs, so that we shall be more capable of instructing our young people in the things they need to learn.**

All: **We are grateful, O God, for the Way of Christ and all there is to explore in it. Make us explorers all of our lives, and let our** experiences confirm to us the importance of this journey. Through Jesus, who has taught us to pray together, saying, "Our Father, who art in heaven . . ."

Suggested readings: 1 Samuel 2:18-21, 26; Proverbs 8; Luke 2:39-51

GRADUATION SUNDAY

Pastoral Prayer

OUR HEARTS ARE LIFTED up, O God, at the sight of young men and women at the point of graduating from high school or college. We know what a significant milestone this is in their lives, and how excited they are to be completing a course of study that allows them to advance now to another segment of their existence. You have made life itself so cunningly, Lord, like a mystery that takes many new turns as we read it. There is always an element of surprise in it, of something that will carry us away from our ordinary experiences and into realms of novelty and discovery. These young people can discern that. They realize that life is about to accelerate for them in some new directions. We thank you for what they have learned thus far about life and themselves. We praise you for their parents, their teachers, and their companions, all of whom have been an important part of their learning process. Now we ask you to prepare them for the new experiences they will encounter—for further education, for meaningful employment, for marriage, for parenthood, for all the broadening, deepening engagements that will greatly influence them in the future. Give them hope in their intelligence and competencies, and give them courage to live with their disappointments. Make them loving and generous toward others, so that they will find the world friendly and comforting. And, above all, teach them what the ancient prophet said is the best way of all, to do justice, to love mercy, and to walk humbly with you, in order that they may fulfill their deepest spiritual obligations to the life they have been given. And we shall all praise you for your eternal love and goodness, through Jesus Christ our Lord. Amen.

Responsive Prayer

Leader: This is an important moment along life's journey, O God, and we join together now to consecrate it to you.

Graduates: **It is by your grace, dear God, that we have come this far in our lives, and we seek your help as we move on from here.**

Leader: We acknowledge all those who have been instrumental in our graduates' lives: their parents, teachers, coaches, friends, siblings, and other relatives.

Graduates: **We would not forget our church, and what it has meant in our development; and we acknowledge your importance, O God, in everything we do.**

Leader: We honor all parents, teachers, and friends of our graduates who are here today, and invite them to join us in this prayer.

All (except the graduates): **We pray for these graduates, dear God, that you will bless them with your heavenly Spirit and keep them from all harm; give them a sense of joy and a sense of responsibility; help them become all that is in them to become; and, above all, let them know that they are loved by you and by us.**

All (including the graduates): **For yours is the wonderful kingdom and the incredible power and the overwhelming glory forever and ever. Amen.**

Suggested readings: 1 Samuel 17:31-51; Psalm 23; Mark 6:1-6

GROUND BREAKING SUNDAY OR DEDICATION OF A NEW OR REFURBISHED BUILDING

Pastoral Prayer

WHEN KING SOLOMON was dedicating his marvelous temple to you, O God, he said that "even heaven and the highest heaven cannot contain you, much less this house that I have built" (1 Kings 8:27). How true that was! Your glory and majesty are too much for any earthly building. You have your dwelling place in the hearts of all the saints and angels who have ever lived, and in our hearts today. Yet in our desire to honor you, and in accommodation to our own earthly need to pay homage through architecture and decoration, we have gathered here today to praise you through the erection (or refurbishment) of another building, which we expect to be hallowed through the coming years by your holy presence and the many lives that will be touched and affected by its existence. It is our offering to you, O God, for all you have done for us and will continue to do in our midst as long as this building shall stand. In this new (redecorated) building, dear Lord, we hope to worship you, visit with you, learn of you, and be commissioned by you to go forth as your witnesses in this place and around the world. We acknowledge before you all those who have already had an intimate part in the erecting (refurnishing) of this edifice: those with the vision to discern its importance and those with the skill to draw up its plans; those who oversaw the financial dimensions of the undertaking; the members of the congregation who have endorsed it and supported it with their gifts and offerings; and the architects, engineers, and workers who (will) have had a part in making it an actuality. We commend to you also those who have prayed for this building and its eventual suitableness as a physical dwelling place for our God. We are a community of believers, O God, devoted to you because of your grace and mercy through many years, and we ask that the erection (refurbishing) of this building will draw us together more closely than ever in your service for the years to come. To that end, may your great name be praised by this ongoing reminder of your importance in our lives, and may we serve you with increasing love and devotion. Through Christ our Lord. Amen.

Responsive Prayer

Leader: It has long been said, O God, that "the clothes make the man"; could it be true as well that "the building makes the congregation"?

People: **We know that you cannot be contained by any earthly building, O Lord; but buildings are expressions of our great regard for you, and help to remind us and our communities of that regard.**

Leader: Therefore we pray that you will forgive us for any presumptuousness attached to what we have undertaken to do in your name, and receive it as our praise for your loving faithfulness to us through all the years.

People: **You have healed our sick, comforted our hearts, sustained us in our most difficult hours, helped us love and forgive our enemies, and given us joy and peace. You have been our rock and our salvation, a heavenly presence in every time of trouble. This building is our way of saying thank you. We love you, God.**

Leader: We ask that you will accept this gesture of our love and faith, and bless it for all time to come, that it may continue to reflect the gratitude and goodwill with which it was offered and thus enrich the lives of future generations.

People: **This is (will be) only a building, a physical manifestation of our regard for you. But we ask that you will accept with it the love and devotion of our hearts, which are your real dwelling place, and enable us to live in constant awareness of your presence here.**

All: **In the name of the Father, Son, and Holy Spirit. Amen.**

Suggested readings: 1 Kings 8:22-30; Psalm 100; Mark 12:41–13:4

ANNIVERSARY SUNDAY

Pastoral Prayer

OUR LIVES REALLY consist of very special moments, O God, linked together over a period of time. Yet the period of time is very important as an envelope for those moments, a track along which we can trace them. That is why anniversaries are significant: they remind us of a period in which meaningful things occurred. And it is why we celebrate today this important anniversary of our church. So much has happened in our community since it was established, O God: little children have been baptized here and have grown and married here and had children of their own; people's lives have been comforted in times of stress or death or hardship; the destinies of some have been changed profoundly by voices they have heard or insights that have come to them here; and we have all been blessed and strengthened by our weekly worship and study in this place. It is hard for us to imagine our lives without this church, dear God, and its inestimable influence on the way we live and move and have our being. We thank you for an opportunity to review the church's importance in our daily existence, and praise you for the spirit and the factors that led to its formation all those years ago. Forgive us for ever taking it for granted—for not remembering the vision and dedication of its founders, or the hard work of all of those who have sustained it through the years, or the gifts of its members who have contributed to its existence since the beginning. As we receive the benefits of their devotion and commitment, help us to take their places in assuming the responsibility for our church's future life. Make us the worthy guardians of their hopes and traditions. Help us to dedicate ourselves to you with the joy and steadfastness that marked their own dedication, and let us worship you with all that we are and all that we have. For you are God, and you have blessed us with your Spirit. Through Jesus Christ our Lord. Amen.

Responsive Prayer

Leader: This is an important day in the life of our church, O God, and we hope to honor you by remembering it.

People: **You have blessed this congregation for many years, and our lives are richer and better because of it.**

Leader: We have worshiped here, found comfort here, baptized our children here, married here, and buried our dead from here.

People: **This church has been extremely significant in our social and spiritual journeys, O God, and we praise you for its existence.**

Leader: Teach us, we pray, to have a profound respect for its history and its place in this community.

People: **Help us to reconsecrate ourselves as the stewards of your grace in this church, and recommit ourselves to the gospel of Christ.**

Leader: Refresh us for our journey as a congregation, and make us open to your will in all things.

People: **Send your Holy Spirit upon us again, that we may be revived as a church and may undertake important roles in the year ahead.**

All: **For you are the God of our salvation, and the giver of hope, and the center of all love. Through Christ our Lord. Amen.**

Suggested readings: Deuteronomy 26:1-11; Psalm 118:1-4, 21-29; Matthew 16:13-20

MEMBERS LEAVING THE COMMUNITY

Pastoral Prayer

FROM TIME IMMEMORIAL, O God, it has been hard to give up friends and family members when they moved away. Even the neighbors of Abraham and Sarah must have regretted seeing them leave Ur of the Chaldees. We feel an inward pain when we have to say goodbye to members of our church who are leaving our community to take up residence in another place. Our hearts are hurting today to have to surrender _____ and _____ and their children _____ and _____, who will be moving this week to their new home in _____. You know how dear they have been to us, O Lord, and to the work and ministry of Christ in this place. We pray for them as they make this important change in their lives, that your Holy Spirit will go with them to watch over them, to prosper them in everything they do, and to keep our hearts united across the years. We ask for them an easy transition, in which they all become quickly adjusted to their new situations. Give them a new life, with equally vital roles, in another Christian community where they can find comfort, strength, and an opportunity to use their many skills and talents. Let them reflect often, in the coming days, on the promise that "all things work together for good for those who love God, who are called according to his purpose" (Romans 8:28), and know that they are always kept in the power and love of our compassionate Father. And grant that we may all live openly and generously, ready to follow your will, wherever it may lead us, with joy and enthusiasm in our spirits. Through Christ our Lord. Amen.

Responsive Prayer

Leader: We live in a highly mobile age, dear God, when people often move to new locations and reestablish life in new connections.

People: **It is always an opportunity to grow, but it is also a threat to our need for security and continuity.**

Leader: Lord, we pray for _____ and _____ and their children _____ and _____ as they leave our community to take up residence in a new place.

People: **Give them strength and comfort for this move, and help them to make their adjustments easily. Bless them with new friends and a sense of joy in their work and play.**

Leader: We pray that they may quickly find new Christian friends who will lead them to a meaningful fellowship in another church, where they will receive nourishment and give themselves with the kind of openness and liberality for which we have known them here.

People: **Help them to meet their new challenges with creativity and know that you are always there to support and guide them. And let them know that they go with our love and blessing to everything that awaits them in their new home.**

All: **To which we all say a hearty "Amen," and send you on your way with hugs and kisses. In the name of the Father, Son, and Holy Spirit. Amen.**

Suggested readings: Genesis 12:1-9; Psalm 86:1-13; 2 Timothy 1:1-12

PERSONS ENTERING
A RETIREMENT HOME

Pastoral Prayer

FOR MOST OF US, O God, life is a long road and has many turnings. One of these comes at the end of a lengthy and productive existence when we decide to leave the responsibilities of a private home and retire to a more convenient dwelling place. We thank you for the combination of foresight and compassion that have led to the development of modern retirement homes, where residents can continue to enjoy their independence in a setting of care and convenience relative to their personal needs. How our ancestors would have loved such a place! Today, dear God, we would like to offer a prayer for our friend(s) _____, who (has, have) reached the point in (his, her, their) journey where (he, she, they) will find new comfort in such a wonderful setting. We know that such moves at any age are fraught with a certain amount of doubt and anxiety, and we pray that _____ may find such immediate joy and relief in (his, her, their) new setting that (he, she, they) will quickly move beyond all sense of hesitance and embrace the delightful possibilities of (his, her, their) life there. Help (him, her, them) always to know that you are (his, her, their) rock of salvation, and a very present help in time of trouble. And let (him, her, them) remember that all (his, her, their) friends are surrounding (him, her, them) with love and prayers during this period of transition, so that (he, she, they) (is, are) never alone. May the comforting power of your Holy Spirit accompany (him, her, them) at every turn and in every moment, to your own pleasure and glory. Through Christ Jesus our Lord. Amen.

Responsive Prayer

Leader: It is never truly easy, dear God, to leave our comfortable homes and all the possessions that remind us of our life and history where we've been.

People: **We pray for our dear friend(s) _____, who (has, have) found the courage and strength to make this important move.**

93

Leader: We ask you to bless (him, her, them) with a special sense of your presence during this time of transition.

People: **Let (his, her, their) faith, that has always been in the triumph of the spiritual life over materialistic things, be especially strong and meaningful now.**

Leader: Grant that this may be such an exciting time of discovery and growth for _____ that (his, her, their) spirit(s) may soon flourish in (his, her, their) new home.

People: **Then we shall all sing your praises, and say again, "What a great God we love and worship!"**

All: **For your name's sake. Amen.**

Suggested readings: Ruth 1:1-18; Isaiah 41:17-20; Luke 2:22-38

SCOUT SUNDAY

Pastoral Prayer

WE ARE PLEASED TODAY, dear God, to honor our young people engaged in the honorable tradition of scouting. We are proud of them, and gladly acknowledge their importance to us and our community. We thank you for their leaders, who give valuable time and effort to convening and training them, and for all who help with their troops in any way. We believe that the values they espouse as scouts come from you, for you have taught us the meaning of discipline, the virtue of work, reverence for life and nature, and the ethics of honesty and trustworthiness. You have shown us, moreover, the importance of caring for others in the community, and for serving them in humble yet meaningful ways. We pray for our own scouts in particular, and for all other scouts as well, here and in other parts of the world, that they may continue to find joy and blessedness in their programs, and that they may grow into adulthood as strong and responsible men and women who will make valuable contributions to their churches, their communities, their countries, and the world. May your Holy Spirit rest upon them to guide them, especially at the more difficult points of their journeys, and bring them happily into your eternal kingdom. For you are our God, and we commend them to you with all of our hearts. Through Jesus Christ our Lord. Amen.

Responsive Prayer

Leader: On this day, O God, we recognize all our young people who participate in the various phases of scouting, and ask you to hear their prayers.

Scouts: **We pray, dear God, for the strength and wisdom to be good and worthy scouts, and to honor you by our service to others in our community.**

Leader: Let your Spirit be upon them to keep them from all harm, to develop their minds, bodies, and spirits, and to accompany them through their life's journeys.

Scouts: **Help us to follow Christ with such faithfulness that we become his obedient servants, embodying his teachings about love and forgiveness.**

Leader: Grant them your special protection in this difficult time in which we live, that they may always choose the exemplary way above all others.

Scouts: **Teach us to know right from wrong and always to elect the right, for the sake of our Lord. And make us witnesses to the gospel of peace in a world that is often in conflict.**

All (including the congregation): **For yours is the kingdom above every kingdom and the power and glory beyond all other power and glory, forever and ever. Amen.**

Suggested readings: Proverbs 4:1-12; Psalm 34:1-10; Matthew 5:1-16

THOSE LEAVING FOR MILITARY SERVICE

Pastoral Prayer

FROM THE BEGINNING of history, O God, young men and women have been called away in the defense of their nations and the causes for which they stood. It is always a sad time for those who watch them go, and often for them as well. But it is also a time of dedication and excitement, for they are going to new experiences that will make them stronger and wiser persons. We pray today for _____ and _____, fine young people from our congregation, who will be leaving this week for service in the U. S. Armed Forces. We ask your loving protection for them, that they will be kept from physical harm and undue stress, and that their experiences will be positive and uplifting. Teach them, in times of pressure, to rely upon your spiritual presence to strengthen and encourage them. Help them, throughout their tour of duty, to be faithful witnesses to Jesus Christ and his teachings, which they have learned from this church and their family. Grant that in all they do and see they may become even more convinced of your unchanging love for them and the world around them, and bring them home again to their families and this community with an enlarged sense of your intimate involvement in our lives. For yours is the kingdom and the power and the glory forever. Amen.

Responsive Prayer

Leader: You are the God of the universe, O Lord, and there is nothing that does not come within the scope of your power.

People: **Therefore we commend to you our friends _____ and _____, who are leaving us to enter the U. S. Armed Forces. Watch over them and keep them, dear God, and be their constant companion.**

Leader: Let your Holy Spirit remind them continually of your loving care, and use them as witnesses to the gospel of Christ wherever they go.

People: **Bless their families while they are away, and keep their minds and hearts in perfect peace.**

Leader: Grant that we, as a church, may continue to uphold both them and their families in prayer and love until they are once again rejoined.

People: **And help us all to live with a constant appreciation of the many soldiers, sailors, and Marines who guard our freedom around the globe, and hold them closely in our thoughts and prayers.**

All: **For you are the Lord of all life, and we offer our prayers in the name of Jesus Christ our Savior. Amen.**

Suggested readings: Judges 6:11-24; Psalm 61; Ephesians 6:10-17

THE BEGINNING OF SUMMER VACATIONS

Pastoral Prayer

IT IS THAT TIME OF year again, O God, when many people head for the beach or the mountains to re-create themselves as families and to rediscover the centers of their lives in a busy world. Even as a congregation, we seem to breathe a sigh of collective relief as schools take a recess and many workplaces drop into lower gear and the days are longer and we can spend more time enjoying the natural world around us. We thank you for the sense of extra peace and tranquillity, and the feeling of well-being that comes from living under less stressful conditions. Forgive us for letting our lives pile up on themselves like the cars of a train that has jumped the track, and help us to use this time to sort ourselves out and reestablish our priorities. Whatever we do, wherever we go, or even if we turn off the telephone and stay home for a while, grant that we shall rediscover your eternal serenity at the center of our lives and then find new health and joy spreading through our minds and beings. Let this be for all of us a season of renewal and growth, a time when we submit ourselves to you anew and find ourselves being transformed in ways that will affect us for the rest of our lives. Protect all of those who travel. Help our children to grow in exciting new ways this summer. Anoint our families with a stronger sense of companionship. Fill our worship services with your Spirit during these months. And let your divine freshness be upon our lives throughout this season and forever. Through Jesus Christ our Lord. Amen.

Responsive Prayer

Leader: Once again, O Lord, we turn to the season of vacations and outdoor activities.

People: **We praise you for the beauty of the world, and for the turning of the seasons that you have ordained.**

Leader: Grant that we shall use the refreshment of this time of the year to find a greater sense of your presence in our lives.

People: **Help us to see you in the beauty of nature, in the activities of the season, and in the faces of our families and friends. Let this be a time when we see more clearly, feel more deeply, and discover you more intimately in everything we do.**

Leader: Protect us in our homes and in our travels.

People: **And keep us mindful of all those in the world who have neither homes nor travels because their lives have not been as fortunate as ours. Teach us to share what we have with them.**

All: **Through Jesus Christ, our loving Lord. Amen.**

Suggested readings: 2 Samuel 7:18-29; Psalm 42; Mark 7:24-30

VACATION BIBLE SCHOOL

Pastoral Prayer

THERE IS EXCITEMENT in the air, O God. Our hearts are lifted up at the sense of something important that is about to happen. A lot of children are going to gather within these walls for several days of special activities. They will sing and learn and play together. Their teachers and leaders will be happy to share this time with them. Your name will be glorified in everything that happens. We shall all have a sense of your presence, and know that something significant is happening in our lives. What happens here will cast its blessing upon the rest of our summer, and even on the rest of our lives. We shall feel your love and care for us more intensely because of these days together. That will affect how we feel about everything—our play, our family lives, our circle of friends, the trips we make, our return to school in the fall, whatever we do. Therefore we thank you and pray for this blessing for every single child who will take part in Vacation Bible School, and for the teachers and leaders as well. Reveal yourself in the very excitement we feel, dear God, and help us to know you as the God of all excitement. For there is nothing in the world more exciting than knowing you. Amen.

Unity Prayer

We are about to begin a very important time in our lives, O God, when we will learn many things about you and how you love us and the world. Be with us as we sing and pray and learn and play. Grant that we may have a very special time together, and that each day will help us to live closer to you. Be with all of those who will lead and teach, and with every single child who attends. Help us to remember children around the world who do not have this opportunity, and to pray for them and their families. And may your Holy Spirit be with us to help us learn and grow. Through our friend and Savior, Jesus Christ. Amen.

Suggested readings: Genesis 6:11-22; Psalm 98; Philippians 2:12-18

HUNDREDTH BIRTHDAY CELEBRATION

Pastoral Prayer

THE BIBLE HAS always given a prominent place to seniors, O God, and we revere them in the church. They bring wisdom, insight, and a knowledge of life and history to our community.

Their age entitles them to say things that others may not say. Their many experiences give weight to their points of view and philosophical conclusions. And their acquaintance with death, sorrow, and illness endows them with a perspective on everything that is often lacking in others. Therefore we praise you for them and their contributions to our fellowship. And today we praise you especially for _____, who will be one hundred years old this week. We thank you for _____'s long life, and for (his, her) wonderful qualities. (List several personal traits.) We pray for _____, that you will continue to give (him, her) health and happiness and clarity of mind. Bless (his, her) friends and family members with a sense of your presence mediated by (him, her). Teach us all to be grateful for our days on this earth, for the people who love us, and for the opportunities of service we are given. Help us to witness to our faith with the kind of loyalty and perseverance we have seen in _____. And grant that we may all look forward beyond this life, as (he, she) does, to a grand reunion with all the saints around your eternal throne. Through Christ Jesus our Lord. Amen.

Responsive Prayer

Leader: We thank you, O God, for the blessings of age.

People: **For the vast experience it brings, for the wisdom distilled from those experiences, and for the sense of having walked with you for so long.**

Leader: We pray today for _____, who is having a hundredth birthday celebration this week.

People: **Give (him, her) a sense of real joy in this achievement, and a feeling of gratitude for life itself.**

Leader: Help us all to be reminded by this happy event of the importance of every day that we live, and of living it in ways that are pleasing to you.

People: **Grant that we may be always loving and caring, and lay up treasures in heaven, where nothing can diminish or destroy them.**

Leader: Teach us never to be greedy or materialistic or selfish or blind to the needs and sufferings of others.

People: **Let us instead be sensitive and compassionate and generous,** and let Christ reign in our hearts at all times, so that when we get to be _____'s age, if we do, we shall experience an enormous satisfaction in everything that has happened in our lives.

All: We pray in his name and for the sake of his everlasting kingdom. Amen.

Suggested readings: Ecclesiastes 3:1-8; Psalm 131; Hebrews 11:1-16

ADOPTION OR BIRTH OF A CHILD

Pastoral Prayer

IN ALL OF HUMAN EXPERIENCE, O God, there is nothing like having a little child come into the home. It changes every-thing completely, for there is something sacred and transcendent about such a bundle of innocence waiting to be shaped and molded by its experiences among us. The joy of a child never deserts us, even if later there may be misunderstandings and hurt feelings. It is a holy privilege to have a child, dear Father, and caring for a child reminds us of the way you care for us. We pray today for _____, who have recently (adopted, given birth to) a child named _____. May your divine blessing rest upon them and (child's name). Grant that the happiness they are feeling in this new relationship may enrich their existence for the rest of their lives. Give them health and strength to care for little _____, and to teach (him, her), and to bring (him, her) into a growing awareness of your presence in their lives. Bless their larger families, that they may experience the joy of little _____ as well. And grant that all of us in this community of faith, who are charged with the responsibility of modeling our beliefs and behavior for the young, may have our consciousness raised by this new child in our midst, so that we will be drawn once again to our duty in Christ Jesus our Lord. For it is in his name that we offer this prayer. Amen.

Responsive Prayer

Leader: We know that Jesus loved children, dear God, and never turned them away when they sought his presence.

People: **Therefore we welcome little children into the warmth and love of our congregation, and congratulate the parents who have added a child to our fellowship.**

Leader: We pray today for _____ and their new child _____, and ask for your richest blessings on them, both in their home and in this church.

People: **Help us to welcome them with open arms, and to remember to pray for them regularly, that they may have the strength and wisdom to grow together happily in this new relationship.**

Leader: Make us responsible witnesses to our faith, that this child, like all other children in our congregation, will grow up with a sound foundation in the faith.

People: **Grant that we and they together may have a constant sense of your divine presence in our lives, and that we may joyfully serve you above every master in the world.**

All: **For you alone have the words of eternal life, O God, and you alone are the Creator and Sustainer of all that we are and have. Through Christ Jesus our Lord. Amen.**

Suggested readings: Genesis 1:24-31; 2:1; Psalm 119:1-16; Colossians 3:1-17

REAFFIRMATION OF MARRIAGE VOWS

Pastoral Prayer

THERE IS NOTHING LIKE the experience of being married, O God, for transforming our lives and perspectives. When we enter into an intimate relationship with another human being who has grown up in a different household with an alternate set of experiences and a DNA totally unlike our own, we are inevitably nudged off-center from the persons we were and expected to be. Sometimes our adjustments are painful, for they demand the surrender of cherished habits, ideals, and expectations. Yet we acknowledge the blessing of this, for two persons are always wiser and stronger than one. And when our negotiations are satisfactory, we are then able to achieve a joy and a happiness that none of us can ever achieve alone. Therefore we pray today for (this, these) couple(s) who have expressed a desire to make a public recommitment to their marriage vows, acknowledging that their lives have been changed by their relationships and wishing to renew their pledges of love and faithfulness. They know far more now about the rewards and the price of a good marriage than they did when they originally said their vows, and they come in that knowledge to say, "I have grown, we have grown, and now, in our new understanding, and with fresh love in our hearts, we want to publicly endorse our relationship and reconfirm our faith in the institution of marriage." Therefore, O God, we ask your richest blessings on them and their home(s). Bless them and their children and other family members with a deep sense of joy in one another. Give them the strength and courage always to persevere in their relationship, loving and forgiving, agreeing and disagreeing, and continuing to grow together in a mutuality transcending all differences in temperament and opinion. Make them very generous with one another, in order that each may have the space for personal growth. Give them sensitivity to one another's needs, and a willingness to be there at all times for one another. Let the presence of Christ reign in their home(s), so that they live in harmony not only with one another but with you and your eternal kingdom. And grant that they may enjoy many more years of happiness together, in which they come to love and appreciate one another even more than they do today, and even more than they can imagine. In Jesus' name. Amen.

Responsive Prayer

Leader: Your Word says, O Lord, that it is good for a man and woman to leave their homes and be married to one another.

Couple(s): **We come to reaffirm our love for one another, and to renew our vows of devotion to one another.**

Leader: Bless them, O God, in this reaffirmation and renewal, and let your Holy Spirit watch over them.

Couple(s): **We acknowledge our differences, and thank God for them, because they contribute to our mutual strength and understanding.**

Leader: Grant that all of us may feel a strengthening of our relationships because of this reaffirmation, and sense a renewal in our own devotion.

Other couples present: **We too are grateful for our marriages, O God, and ask you to bless them for the years ahead. May we remain loving and faithful to one another and to you.**

All: **For yours is the kingdom and the power and the glory forever. Amen.**

Suggested readings: Song of Solomon 8:6-7; Psalm 66:8-20; John 2:1-11

RECEPTION OF NEW STAFF MEMBERS

Pastoral Prayer

WE PRAISE YOU, O God, for all of the Christian workers we have known over the years and what they still mean to our lives. And now we rejoice in the addition of new members to the staff of this church, whose presence will strengthen the work of the congregation and enhance our sense of your kingdom in this place. We pray for _____ and _____ and the tasks they will undertake in our midst. Grant them patience with themselves and with us as they begin to learn who we are and how they can best serve your people with their own particular gifts. Help us to be receptive and encouraging to them, so that they will feel welcome and free to use their gifts in this place. Bless the friendships they will form in the days ahead, and let those friendships enrich and enlarge their lives as well as ours. Grant that the freshness they bring to our work will enable all of us to feel renewed and excited about our mission. Let your Holy Spirit use us together to create a stronger witness to your kingdom in this community, so that your name will be glorified and we shall praise you without ceasing. Through Jesus Christ our Lord. Amen.

Responsive Prayer

Leader: In your goodness and wisdom, O God, you have led _____ and _____ to our congregation and will use them to bless our fellowship.

People: **We pray for them to feel happy and welcome here, and to know that we shall appreciate everything they do to make our church a finer and happier community.**

Leader: We do not expect them to be superhuman, O God, or to perform impossible tasks.

People: **But we do ask that we shall make it possible by our love and acceptance for them to do their best at everything they have been trained to do, and thereby help us do all the things that we are able to do.**

Leader: May your loving Spirit abide with all of us, enabling us to be the church you most want us to be.

People: **And may Christ be glorified in all our efforts, that your kingdom may come on earth and all people praise you, days without end.**

All: **Through Jesus our Lord. Amen.**

Suggested readings: Exodus 6:28–7:7; Psalm 8; Acts 16:1-5

MEETING OF THE CONGREGATION

Pastoral Prayer

FROM THE BEGINNING, O God, you ordained that the church should be a gathering of believers in which all have a voice. Eventually this would become the pattern of modern democracy, coming to this country by way of the Pilgrims and their colony in New England. We are grateful for this, because it reminds us of how important each and every one of us is in your sight. Whenever we gather as a congregation, it is as if you are presiding at a town hall meeting and we have an opportunity to voice our ideas, our concerns, and our gratitude to you. We invoke your presence at our meeting today, and ask that your Holy Spirit will anoint our hearts and minds so that we may join together in love and unity to deliberate on matters that concern this local church. Help us to think clearly and to speak humbly and truthfully about everything. Let the mind of Jesus predominate in all that is said and done. If there are things we have not considered but need to consider now, bring them to our attention during this time. If our church has failed to follow Christ in any way, we need to be reminded of that. Above all, dear God, we want to reflect the compassion and redemption of your Spirit, and ask that you will forgive us where we have fallen short and direct us into the paths of righteousness for your name's sake. Through Christ our Lord. Amen.

Responsive Prayer

Leader: There are many voices in the world, dear God, but it is yours we want to hear above all others.

People: **Come and be present now as we meet together as a congregation. Let your Spirit move in our midst, stirring our hearts and minds to renewal and preparing us for the reports and conversations that will occur.**

Leader: Save us from exercises of prejudice and self-assertion, and let us speak always in the interest of others and your kingdom.

People: **Make us wise beyond our own wisdom, and compassionate as Christ was compassionate.**

Leader: Give us an appreciation for all who work hard in the service of this congregation, and for the ministry of this church to all who come here.

People: **Save us from making any decisions that do not reflect your kingdom, and grant that we shall give honor and glory to you through everything we say and do.**

All: **For yours is the kingdom and the power and the glory forever and ever. Amen.**

Suggested readings: Exodus 19:16-25; Psalm 48; John 15:1-14

INSTALLATION OF NEW OFFICERS

Pastoral Prayer

THE BIBLE TELLS US, O God, that one of the first things the early church did after Jesus ascended into heaven was to elect new officers to serve the body of Christ. In that venerable tradition, we come today to install our own new church officers and to ask your blessings on them and the congregation they will serve. We think we know these officers and what they are like. But you know them even more intimately than we do, O God. We pray therefore that you will anoint them with your Holy Spirit to lead them into the most imaginative and productive work of which they are capable. Give them unbounded energy and enthusiasm for their tasks. Help them to be sensitive not only to the feelings of others but to the needs of our congregation and the world we serve. In the words of the ancient prophet, let them do justly, love mercy, and walk humbly with you. Let their responsibility bind them more closely to you, so that they inevitably become more spiritual in their daily living. Grant that their relations with one another will be strong and healthy, and that they will challenge one another to do their very best. We ask you to bless their families, that they too will grow through their experiences. For many of these officers, dear God, their labor for the church will mean a sacrifice of personal time and energy. But we remember that we serve a Lord who sacrificed everything in our behalf. Therefore we offer this prayer in his name, and for the sake of the kingdom he preached. Amen.

Responsive Prayer

Leader: In a world where most people are already busier than they'd like to be, O God, we are grateful for those who are able and willing to serve as officers and leaders of our congregation.

People: **We ask your special blessing on each of them as they undertake their sacred duties. Give them wisdom and health and strength for all the things they must do.**

Leader: Grant that all of us may support them enthusiastically as they assume their positions, and respond to their leadership with joy and thanksgiving.

People: **Help us to hold them up in our prayers and befriend them in every way we can. Let them know that we appreciate what they are doing, and are grateful for the ongoing work of this congregation.**

Leader: Show us how to be better Christians, and to be more sensitive to others and to the ministry of this church in the world.

People: **Teach us to live as Jesus lived, and to fulfill his teachings in our daily existence. Make us an easy people to lead because we are eagerly seeking to do your will.**

All: **And grant that we may love one another so much in Christ that our very existence as a church will prove redemptive in our whole community. Through Jesus our Lord. Amen.**

Suggested readings: Hosea 11:1-4; Psalm 125; Acts 2:43-47

NEW MEMBERS

Pastoral Prayer

IN THE HISTORY OF the world, O God, two things are dearest to us: the coming of Christ and the long existence of the church. The church is really the lengthened shadow of Christ himself.

Therefore it is always of great importance to us when new members are received into our fellowship, for they help extend the life and ministry of Christ in our time. We thank you that in your providence you have brought these members to us and inclined their hearts to become a part of our community of believers. We pray for them as they unite with us, and ask that we may not only receive them warmly now but continue to care for them and their needs in the body of Christ. Help us to listen to them, encourage them, and provide a place of service for them. Grant that they shall be able quickly to form friendships within the congregation that will strengthen them and their new friends as well. As they join us, O God, we are reminded of the challenge that always exists for us, to provide the kind of worship, fellowship, educational program, and opportunities for service that will enable our members to find fulfillment in their individual Christian lives. Therefore we ask that the coming of these new members may inspire our leaders once again to review who we are and how we address the challenge of being church in these times of rapid change, and, having assessed our situation, to do everything we can to be the church you want us to be. To that end, dear God, may your Holy Spirit preside over all the work and meetings of this congregation, to guide, inspire, and strengthen us in the ministry of Christ. For we ask it in our Savior's name. Amen.

Responsive Prayer

Leader: This is your church, O God, and not ours. Therefore we are always seeking to know and follow your will in our affairs.

People: **We thank you for the new members you have led to unite with us today, and for the contributions they will make to the life and ministry of our congregation.**

Leader: We accept the responsibility of loving and caring for them, Father, and for providing for their growth and education in the ministry of Christ.

People: **Grant that their coming will make all of us stronger and more responsible. Teach us to be the church Jesus wanted us to be when he said to Simon Peter about his confession of faith, "On this rock I will build my church."**

Leader: Bless our new friends in all their relationships—with their schools, their neighborhoods, their work, and the entire community.

People: **Help us to continue to pray for them beyond this day, that you will give them joy in this fellowship and that your Holy Spirit will guide and direct them in all things.**

All: **Through Christ our Lord. Amen.**

Suggested readings: Jeremiah 1:4-10; Psalm 146; 2 Corinthians 6:1–7:1

SPECIAL EMPHASIS WEEK

Pastoral Prayer

YOU KNOW, O GOD, what frail and ordinary creatures we are, and how we fall into deadly routines in our lives. Our old habits grow over our strongest and most creative impulses like vines over a garden, and we cease to feel new feelings and act on our highest motivations. Therefore we need special times in our year when we break out of our habitual beings and discover new prospects and new depths in ourselves. This is such a time in the life of our congregation, O God—a time for shedding those immobilizing vines that have grown over us and breaking out of the mold. A time for hearing new thoughts in new voices and learning new music for our hearts to sing. A time for moving beyond our usual boundaries and exploring the life beyond them. A time for hearing you speak to us in new accents, and for yielding to your voice with new eagerness and new obedience. We seek your richest blessing on these days and on those who will lead us in these events. May it be a time of challenge and resensitization for them as well as for us. Send your Holy Spirit on us to open our hearts and minds to the hundreds of possibilities before us, and to fill us with warmth and joy not only in ourselves but in the fellowship of other believers and followers. Let Christ live in us in new ways this week. Let his teachings become alive to us with new vividness and new command. Let his ministry of love and sacrifice grip us as it has not gripped us in a long time.

And let his resurrected presence confront us as it confronted those first disciples in the upper room and remind us, "As the Father has sent me, now I am sending you." For this is an important time, O Father. It is a vital time. It is your time, and we want to be there in it. For Christ's sake. Amen.

Responsive Prayer

Leader: For some of us, O Lord, this will be the most important week of our lives.

People: **It will be a time of new insights and new commitments, a time when our old way of being is challenged and we find the courage to leave it behind for something new and more fulfilling.**

Leader: We need your Spirit in our midst for this to happen.

People: **Some of us need to be shaken to our depths, dear God, so that we come face to face with ourselves and make important decisions about who we are going to be.**

Leader: Others need to find their way quietly back to the path where their lives are serene and productive.

People: **Help us to commit enough of ourselves to this experience to make a difference in us. We would like to see Christ at work in us and our congregation, and be reminded of the most important things we know.**

Leader: To that end, O God, come among us in some very tangible and identifiable ways this week.

People: **Enable us to climb to the mountaintop again, or at least to some high hill, where we can see life as it ought to be and find our true direction once more.**

All: **For you have the compass, Lord. You have the map. You have the words of life. And you are the God of heaven and earth. Through Jesus Christ our Lord. Amen.**

Suggested readings: Exodus 20:18-24; Psalm 42; Galatians 5:16-26

POTLUCK SUPPER

Pastoral Prayer

WE KNOW WHY WE call them "potluck suppers," O God—because when we have them we take the luck of the pots and whatever is in them. But we also know that our pots are some of the best in the world, and we can never come together over such sumptuous feasts without being haunted by the specter of all the tables in the world where there is not much food, or even of homes too poor to have a table. Therefore we come together with a profound sense of gratitude that we happen to live in a land of plenty where there is a tradition of bounty and our tables always resemble something out of *Southern Living* magazine. We cannot fail to lift up our prayers for those whose plates are bare and whose larders are always empty. We know it is only by accident of birth and not through any divine plan that we have a surplus of food while they have almost nothing. Therefore we ask two things of you, dear Father. We ask that we may live as gratefully as our abundance requires, without letting a single meal go by when we do not either mentally or openly give thanks of a very genuine nature. And we ask that we may be prompted, out of our abundance, to share what we have with others. Teach us not to accept the status quo in the world, but to use our sensitivity and articulateness to support the kind of earnest charitable action that will help address the great inequities in the global order. Make us as keen to feed the masses of the world as we are to have clean air and water in our own communities, or to elect the particular political parties we favor. And having made these sober prayers, we now ask your blessing upon the meal we shall eat and upon all the beautiful hands that prepared it and served it and will clean up after us when we are through. In the name of Jesus the Servant. Amen.

Responsive Prayer

Leader: A dinner like this is always a wonderful experience, O God, when we gather around festive tables, share good food, and take delight in one another's company.

People: **Thank you for the bounty of the food and for the talents of the cooks.**

Leader: Help us to eat wisely but enjoy every mouthful we eat.

People: **Let us remember that our bodies are the temples of your Holy Spirit, so that we never abuse them by what we take into them and are always grateful in a spiritual way for everything we have.**

Leader: Give us strength and health for living as your witnesses and bringing joy and happiness to others.

People: **And let the ministry of Christ in word and deed be extended through us to the world, for yours is the kingdom and the power and the glory forever. Amen.**

Suggested readings: 1 Samuel 21:1-6; Psalm 25:4-7; Mark 6:30-44

GOING BACK TO SCHOOL

Pastoral Prayer

OUR LIVES ARE MARKED, O God, by the changing of the seasons. We take unusual delight in these times, for they are periods of heightened expectancy and new growth. It has been a long and busy summer. We have exulted in our various activities. And now it is time to prepare for the fall and winter, and many are going back to school, some here at home and others at a distance. We thank you for all the good events of the summer months—for work and play and relaxation, for fun and friendships and frivolity, for trips to the lake or the beach or the mountains, for a chance to unwind and experience more leisure time. Now we thank you for all the good events that lie ahead—for exciting classes and new friends and ball games and plays and concerts and a raft of holidays. We pray for all our students at every level, and ask that this may be a good year for them. Let their learning be rewarding as well as challenging, and let them enjoy the growth that comes from new experiences. Give them spirits of joy and confidence, and help them to live gratefully at all times, aware of the gift of life and its incredible richness. Bless their teachers and coaches and counselors, and all others who are involved in their educational process. And grant that all of us may share the excitement of the season, whether we are in school or not. For you have made our world extraordinarily beautiful and fascinating, and we are happy to praise you for everything through Christ our Lord. Amen.

Responsive Prayer

Leader: There is always something wonderful about returning to school, O God. Even those of us who no longer go to school remember it fondly at this time of the year.

People: **Seeing old friends again, meeting new ones, having good teachers, going to ball games, exploring new subjects—it is always exciting and promising because it opens new vistas in our lives.**

Leader: We thank you for the opportunity of pursuing our education. Learning is one of the great privileges of life.

People: **We are grateful for chances to grow all of our lives, and to develop constantly into wiser and better persons.**

Leader: We pray that you will help us to seek renewal of our selves in this new season.

People: **Let your Holy Spirit challenge us to new goals and achievements in our spiritual lives, so that we may become the persons you have intended us to be.**

Leader: Teach us the things Jesus knew about love and service and sacrifice.

People: **And show us how to share our wonderful lives with other people who have been less fortunate than we, so that together we may attain your kingdom,**

All: **And rejoice in your power and your glory, through Jesus Christ our Savior. Amen.**

Suggested readings: Job 37:14-24; Psalm 131; Luke 2:39-40, 52

CHRISTMAS CONCERT

Pastoral Prayer

THERE IS LITTLE MUSIC that thrills us more, O God, than the music of Christmas. We thank you for the repertory of this beautiful music that has grown so magnificently through the centuries—for ancient plainsong and hymns and carols from all over the world that now enrich our experience of Advent and Christmas as few things do. We are grateful to you for the musicians of this church and community who work so hard each year to provide us with glorious concerts and keep the experience of this repertory alive. We pray that as we listen again to one of these special concerts our hearts will be appropriately warmed and lifted and we shall find ourselves transported once more to that entrancing scene where Christ was born and the history of the world was suddenly changed. Grant that in the midst of all the rush and busyness of this important season we shall not fail to be quiet and remember the reason it is important. Send your Holy Spirit upon us as you sent it to young Mary, the mother of Jesus, so that we become warmed in our hearts and renewed in our faith. Let hope burn like a candle in the gloom of our despairing world, and light people's way once more to the Savior who was born in a stable in Bethlehem. And as we listen to our choirs and musicians this Christmas, let us imagine that we are actually hearing the angels as they sang at his birth, calling us to devotion as they called the shepherds all those centuries ago. For this is no ordinary time and the music is no ordinary music, and your love for the world overflows in the person of Christ. Amen.

Responsive Prayer

Leader: Our hearts are filled with love and beauty at this time of the year, O God.

People: **Our spirits are captivated once again by the story of the Child of Bethlehem and what he has meant to the world.**

Leader: We thank you for the place that music has in our celebration of Christmas, and the way it reminds us of the music of the angels.

People: **Bless our musicians as they help us to prepare for the coming of Christ in our own time, and make us especially receptive to their ministry today (tonight).**

Leader: Let the One who was born in Bethlehem descend to us again.

People: **Grant that he may bring joy to those who mourn and gladness to those who despaired.**

All: **And let us all see the light shining in the darkness and experience a rebirth of hope. Through Christ our Savior. Amen.**

Suggested readings: Isaiah 40:1-5; Psalm 51:1-14; John 1:1-14